WORLD OF ANIMALS

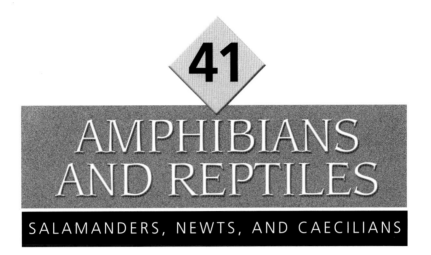

41

AMPHIBIANS AND REPTILES

SALAMANDERS, NEWTS, AND CAECILIANS

Hellbender, Mudpuppy, Lungless
Salamanders, Newts...

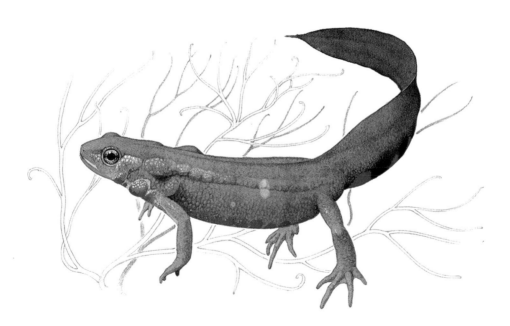

CHRIS MATTISON

GROLIER

an imprint of

SCHOLASTIC

www.scholastic.com/librarypublishing

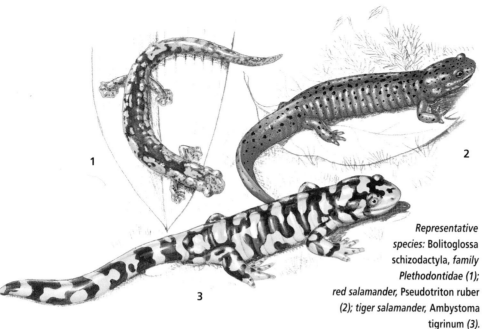

Representative species: Bolitoglossa schizodactyla, *family Plethodontidae (1); red salamander,* Pseudotriton ruber *(2); tiger salamander,* Ambystoma tigrinum *(3).*

Published 2005 by Grolier, an imprint of
Scholastic Library Publishing
Danbury, CT 06816

This edition published exclusively for the school and library market

The Brown Reference Group plc.
(incorporating Andromeda Oxford Limited)
8 Chapel Place
Rivington Street
London
EC2A 3DQ

Library of Congress Cataloging-in-Publication Data

Amphibians and Reptiles.
    p. cm. -- (World of Animals; v. 41-50)
    Contents: [1] Salamanders, newts, and caecilians / Chris Mattison -- [2] Frogs and toads 1 / Chris Mattison -- [3] Frogs and toads 2 / Chris Mattison -- [4] Lizards 1 / Valerie Davies, Chris Mattison -- [5] Lizards 2 / Chris Mattison -- [6] Lizards 3 / Valerie Davies, Chris Mattison -- [7] Turtles and crocodilians / David Alderton -- [8] Snakes 1 / Chris Mattison -- [9] Snakes 2 / Chris Mattison -- [10] Snakes 3 / Chris Mattison.
    ISBN 0-7172-5916-1 (set : alk. paper) -- ISBN 0-7172-5917-X (v. 1 : alk. paper) -- ISBN 0-7172-5918-8 (v. 2 : alk. paper) -- ISBN 0-7172-5919-6 (v. 3 : alk. paper) -- ISBN 0-7172-5920-X (v. 4 : alk. paper) -- ISBN 0-7172-5921-8 (v. 5 : alk. paper) -- ISBN 0-7172-5922-6 (v. 6 : alk. paper) -- ISBN 0-7172-5923-4 (v. 7 : alk. paper) -- ISBN 0-7172-5924-2 (v. 8 : alk. paper) -- ISBN 0-7172-5925-0 (v. 9 : alk. paper) -- ISBN 0-7172-5926-9 (v. 10 : alk. paper)
    1. Amphibians -- Juvenile literature. 2. Reptiles -- Juvenile literature [1. Amphibians. 2. Reptiles.] I. Grolier (Firm) II. Series: World of Animals (Danbury, Conn.); v. 41-50.
QL49.W877 2003
590--dc22
        2002073860

Project Directors: Graham Bateman, Lindsey Lowe
Editors: Virginia Carter, Angela Davies
Art Editor and Designer: Steve McCurdy
Picture Manager: Becky Cox
Picture Researcher: Alison Floyd
Main Artists: Denys Ovenden, Philip Hood, Myke Taylor, Ken Oliver, Michael Woods, David M. Dennis
Maps: Steve McCurdy, Tim Williams
Production: Alastair Gourlay, Maggie Copeland

Printed in Singapore

Set ISBN 0-7172-5916-1

About This Volume

This is the first volume in the *World of Animals* series to deal with amphibians, for which there is a general introduction. There then follows detailed information on caecilians, newts, and salamanders. Caecilians are wormlike amphibians that come from tropical regions on several continents. Most live in burrows, but a few are aquatic. Some lay eggs, while others are live-bearers; but otherwise little is known about their life histories. Salamanders are more familiar: Nine of the 10 families are found in North America, including some of the most interesting species such as the hellbenders, the mudpuppies, and the amphiumas. A number of cave salamanders also live in North America, leading secretive lives in underground rivers and streams and about which next to nothing is known. Others, such as the newts and the mole salamanders, are far easier to find—at least in spring when they visit ponds to breed.

Salamanders have several unique characteristics, including the ability of some populations to breed while still in the larval stage. They grow to adult size while retaining larval characteristics such as gills and fins. In fact, some species, such as the sirens, never metamorphose and are genetically programmed to remain larvae for their entire lives. Others, like some tiger salamanders, are more flexible, with just a proportion of them retaining larval features.

Contents

The three-lined salamander, Eurycea guttolineata from southeastern North America, grows to 7 inches (18 cm) long.

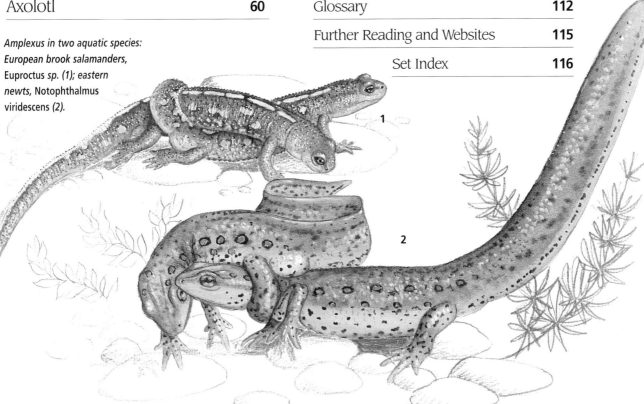

Amplexus in two aquatic species: European brook salamanders, Euproctus sp. (1); eastern newts, Notophthalmus viridescens (2).

1

2

How to Use This Set

World of Animals: Amphibians and Reptiles is a 10-volume set that describes in detail reptiles and amphibians from all corners of the earth. Each volume brings together those animals that are most closely related and have similar lifestyles. So all the frogs and toads are in Volumes 42 and 43, the snakes are in Volumes 48, 49, and 50, and so on. To help you find volumes that interest you, look at pages 6 and 7 (Find the Animal). A brief introduction to each volume is also given on page 2 (About This Volume).

Article Styles

Each volume contains two types of article. The first kind introduces major groups (such as amphibians, reptiles, frogs and toads, or lizards). It presents a general overview of the subject.

The second type of article makes up most of each volume. It describes in detail individual species, such as the American bullfrog or the American alligator, or groups of very similar animals, such as reed frogs or day geckos. Each article starts with a fact-filled **data panel** to help you gather information at a glance. Used together, the two different styles of article will enable you to become familiar with animals in the context of their evolutionary history and biological relationships.

Data panel presents basic statistics of each animal

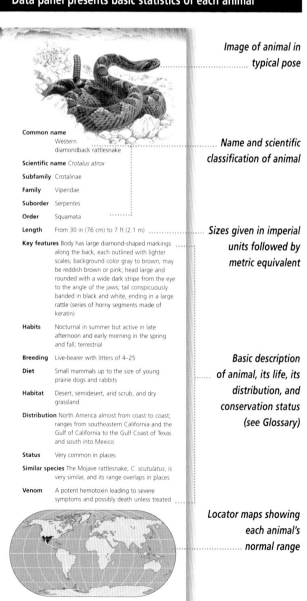

Image of animal in typical pose

Common name Western diamondback rattlesnake

Scientific name *Crotalus atrox*

Subfamily Crotalinae

Family Viperidae

Suborder Serpentes

Order Squamata

Name and scientific classification of animal

Length From 30 in (76 cm) to 7 ft (2.1 m)

Sizes given in imperial units followed by metric equivalent

Key features Body has large diamond-shaped markings along the back, each outlined with lighter scales; background color gray to brown, may be reddish brown or pink; head large and rounded with a wide dark stripe from the eye to the angle of the jaws; tail conspicuously banded in black and white, ending in a large rattle (series of horny segments made of keratin)

Habits Nocturnal in summer but active in late afternoon and early morning in the spring and fall; terrestrial

Breeding Live-bearer with litters of 4–25

Diet Small mammals up to the size of young prairie dogs and rabbits

Habitat Desert, semidesert, arid scrub, and dry grassland

Distribution North America almost from coast to coast; ranges from southeastern California and the Gulf of California to the Gulf Coast of Texas and south into Mexico

Status Very common in places

Similar species The Mojave rattlesnake, *C. scutulatus*, is very similar, and its range overlaps in places

Venom A potent hemotoxin leading to severe symptoms and possibly death unless treated

Basic description of animal, its life, its distribution, and conservation status (see Glossary)

Locator maps showing each animal's normal range

Article describes a particular animal

Scientific name of animal

Common name of animal

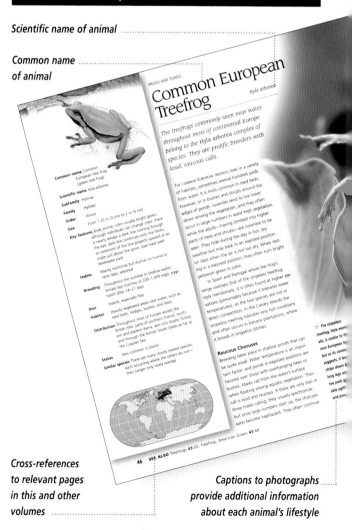

FROGS AND TOADS

Common European Treefrog

Hyla arborea

The treefrogs commonly seen near water throughout most of continental Europe belong to the Hyla arborea complex of species. They are prolific breeders with loud, raucous calls.

THE COMMON EUROPEAN TREEFROG lives in a variety of habitats, sometimes several hundred yards from water. It is most common in reed beds, however, or in bushes and shrubs around the edges of ponds. Juveniles tend to live lower down among the vegetation, and they often occur in large numbers in waist-high vegetation, while the adults—having climbed into higher parts of trees and shrubs—are nowhere to be seen. They hide during the day in hot, dry weather but may bask in an exposed position on days when the air is not too dry. When resting in an exposed position, they often turn bright yellowish green in color.

In Spain and Portugal where the frog's range overlaps that of the stripeless treefrog, *Hyla meridionalis*, it is often found at higher elevations (presumably because it tolerates lower temperatures), so the two species are not in direct competition. In the Canary Islands the stripeless treefrog tolerates very hot conditions and often occurs in banana plantations, where it breeds in irrigation ditches.

Raucous Choruses
Breeding takes place in shallow ponds that can be quite small. Water temperature is an important factor, and ponds in exposed positions are favored over those with the water's surface shaded by overhanging trees or bushes. Males call from the water's edge when floating among aquatic vegetation. Their call is loud and raucous. If there are only two or three males calling, they usually synchronize; but once large numbers start up, the choruses soon become haphazard. They often continue

Common name Common European tree frog (green tree frog)

Scientific name *Hyla arborea*

Subfamily Hylinae

Family Hylidae

Order Anura

Size From 1.25 in (3 cm) to 2 in (5 cm)

Key features Body plump; color usually bright green, although individuals can change color; there is nearly always a dark line running through the eye; dark line continues onto the flanks, an extension of the line projects upward at an angle just above the groin; toes have well-developed pads

Habits Mainly nocturnal but diurnal on humid or rainy days; arboreal

Breeding Throughout the summer in shallow water; female lays clutches of 200–1,400 eggs; eggs hatch after 14–21 days

Diet Insects, especially flies

Habitat Heavily vegetated areas near water, such as reed beds, hedges, bushes, and trees

Distribution Throughout most of Europe except the British Isles, parts of southern France, southern and eastern Iberia, also into Asiatic Turkey and through the former Soviet states as far as the Caspian Sea

Status Very common in places

Similar species There are many closely related species, each occurring where the others do not—their ranges only rarely overlap

⊕ *The stripeless treefrog, Hyla meridionalis, is similar to the Common European treefrog but as its common name suggests, it lacks the stripe down each flank; its long legs and large toe pads give it remarkable agility and grip.*

SEE ALSO Treefrogs 43:32, Treefrog, American Green 43:48

46

Cross-references to relevant pages in this and other volumes

Captions to photographs provide additional information about each animal's lifestyle

A number of other features help you navigate through the volumes and present you with helpful extra information. At the bottom of many pages are **cross-references** to other articles of interest. They may be to related animals, animals that live in similar places, or that have similar behavior, predators (or prey), lifestyles, and much more. Each volume also contains a **Set Index** to the complete *World of Animals: Amphibians and Reptiles*. Animals mentioned in the text are indexed by common and scientific names, and many topics are also covered. There is also a **Glossary** that will help you understand certain technical words. Each volume includes lists of useful **Further Reading and Websites** that help you take your research further.

Introductory article describes family or closely related groups

Graphic full-color photographs bring text to life

Easy-to-read and comprehensive text

Detailed diagrams illustrate text

Tables summarize classification of groups

Who's Who tables summarize classification of each major group

Introductory article describes major groups of animals

At-a-glance boxes cover topics of special interest

Meticulous drawings illustrate a typical selection of group members

Find the Animal

World of Animals: Amphibians and Reptiles is the fifth part of a library that describes all groups of living animals. Each cluster of volumes in *World of Animals* covers a familiar group of animals—mammals, birds, reptiles and amphibians, fish, and insects and other invertebrates.

The Animal Kingdom

The living world is divided into five kingdoms, one of which (kingdom Animalia) is the main subject of the *World of Animals*. Kingdom Animalia is divided into major groups called phyla. The phylum Chordata contains those animals that have a backbone—mammals, birds, reptiles, amphibians, and fish. Animals without backbones (so-called invertebrates, such as insects, spiders, mollusks, and crustaceans) belong to many different phyla. To find which set of volumes in the *World of Animals* you need, see the chart below.

World of Animals: Amphibians and Reptiles deals with two of the oldest lineages of land animals—the amphibians, which evolved from fish some 400 million years ago, and the reptiles, which evolved from amphibians about 350 million years ago. Although they are no longer dominant animals on earth (unlike the early reptiles typified by the dinosaurs), over 5,000 amphibian species and 8,000 species of reptiles can still be found. Most live in warmer or tropical regions of the world.

Rank	Scientific name	Common name
Kingdom	Animalia	Animals
Phylum	Chordata	Animals with a backbone
Class	Reptilia	Reptiles
Order	Squamata	Lizards, Snakes, Amphisbaenians
Suborder	Serpentes	Snakes
Family	Viperidae	Vipers and Pit Vipers
Genus	*Crotalus*	Rattlesnakes
Species	*Crotalus atrox*	Western diamondback rattlesnake

The kingdom Animalia is subdivided into phyla, classes, orders, families, genera, and species. Above is the classification for the western diamondback rattlesnake.

All western diamondback rattlesnakes look alike, breed together, and produce young like themselves. This distinction corresponds closely to the zoologists' definition of a species.

Zoologists use an internationally recognized system for naming species consisting of two-word scientific names, usually in Latin or Greek. The western diamondback rattlesnake is called *Crotalus atrox,* and the sidewinder *Crotalus cerastes. Crotalus* is the name of the genus (a group of very similar species); *atrox* or *cerastes* indicates the species in the genus. The same scientific names are recognized the world over. However, a species

⊕ *This chart lists the phyla in two of the five kingdoms. The phylum Arthropoda makes up a high proportion of all invertebrate animals.*

Naming Animals

To discuss animals, names are needed for the different kinds. Western diamondback rattlesnakes are one kind of snake, and sidewinders are another.

⊕ *The main groups of animals alive today. Volumes that cover each major group are indicated below.*

ANIMALS
Kingdom Animalia

SINGLE-CELLED LIFE
Kingdom Protista

Vertebrates/ Chordates
Phylum Chordata

Invertebrates
Numerous Phyla

Mammals Class Mammalia	**Birds** Class Aves	**Reptiles** Class Reptilia	**Amphibians** Class Amphibia	**Fish** Several classes	**Insects, spiders, mollusks, spiny-skinned animals, worms**	**Single-Celled Life**
Volumes 1–10	*Volumes 11–20*	*Volumes 44–50*	*Volumes 41–43*	*Volumes 31–40*	*Volumes 21–30*	*Volume 21 (part)*

Groups of Amphibians and Reptiles

CLASS: AMPHIBIA—AMPHIBIANS

ORDER: Gymnophiona (Vol. 41) — caecilians
ORDER: Caudata (Vol. 41) — salamanders and newts
ORDER: Anura (Vols. 42–43) — frogs and toads
   Family: Ascaphidae (Vol. 42) — tailed frogs
   Family: Leiopelmatidae (Vol. 42) — New Zealand frogs
   Family: Bombinatoridae (Vol. 42) — fire-bellied toads
   Family: Discoglossidae (Vol. 42) — painted frogs and midwife toads
   Family: Megophryidae (Vol. 42) — Asian horned toads and litter frogs
   Family: Pelobatidae (Vol. 42) — spadefoot toads
   Family: Pelodytidae (Vol. 42) — parsley frogs
   Family: Pipidae (Vol. 42) — clawed and Surinam toads
   Family: Rhinophrynidae (Vol. 42) — Mexican burrowing frogs
   Family: Heleophrynidae (Vol. 43) — ghost frogs
   Family: Myobatrachidae (Vol. 42) — southern frogs and Australian toadlets
   Family: Sooglossidae (Vol. 43) — Seychelles frogs
   Family: Leptodactylidae (Vol. 42) — rain frogs
   Family: Bufonidae (Vol. 42) — true toads and harlequin toads
   Family: Brachycephalidae (Vol. 42) — three-toed toadlets
   Family: Dendrobatidae (Vol. 43) — poison dart frogs
   Family: Rhinodermatidae (Vol. 43) — gastric-brooding frogs
   Family: Hylidae (Vol.43) — treefrogs, marsupial frogs, and leaf frogs
   Family: Pseudidae (Vol. 43) — paradoxical frogs
   Family: Centrolenidae (Vol. 43) — glass frogs
   Family: Allophrynidae (Vol. 43) — no common name
   Family: Ranidae (Vol. 43) — water frogs
   Family: Arthroleptidae (Vol. 43) — bush squeakers
   Family: Hemisotidae (Vol. 43) — shovel-nosed frogs
   Family: Hyperoliidae (Vol. 43) — reed frogs and relatives
   Family: Rhacophoridae (Vol. 43) — Afro-Asian treefrogs
   Family: Mantellidae (Vol. 43) — Madagascan frogs
   Family: Microhylidae (Vol. 42) — narrow-mouthed frogs

CLASS: REPTILIA—REPTILES

ORDER: Squamata—lizards, snakes, and amphisbaenians
Suborder: Sauria (Vols. 44–46) — lizards
   Family: Agamidae (Vol. 44) — agamas and dragon lizards
   Family: Chamaeleonidae (Vol. 44) — chameleons and dwarf chameleons
   Family: Iguanidae (Vol. 44) — iguanas, basilisks, collared lizards, and anoles
   Family: Gekkonidae (Vol. 45) — "typical" geckos
   Family: Diplodactylidae (Vol. 45) — southern geckos
   Family: Pygopodidae (Vol. 45) — flap-footed lizards
   Family: Eublepharidae (Vol. 45) — eyelid geckos
   Family: Teiidae (Vol. 45) — tegus, whiptails, and racerunners
   Family: Gymnophthalmidae (Vol. 45) — spectacled lizards
   Family: Lacertidae (Vol. 45) — wall lizards
   Family: Xantusiidae (Vol. 45) — night lizards
   Family: Scincidae (Vol. 46) — skinks
   Family: Gerrhosauridae (Vol. 45) — plated lizards
   Family: Cordylidae (Vol. 45) — girdle-tailed lizards
   Family: Dibamidae (Vol. 45) — blind lizards
   Family: Xenosauridae (Vol. 46) — knob-scaled and crocodile lizards
   Family: Anguidae (Vol. 46) — alligator and glass lizards
   Family: Varanidae (Vol. 46) — monitor lizards
   Family: Helodermatidae (Vol. 46) — beaded lizards
   Family: Lanthonotidae (Vol. 46) — Borneo earless monitor

Suborder: Amphisbaenia (Vol. 46) — amphisbaenians (worm lizards)
Suborder: Serpentes (Vols. 48–50) — snakes
   Family: Anomalepidae (Vol. 48) — dawn blind snakes
   Family: Leptotyphlopidae (Vol. 48) — thread snakes
   Family: Typhlopidae (Vol. 48) — blind snakes
   Family: Anomochilidae (Vol. 48) — dwarf pipe snakes
   Family: Uropeltidae (Vol. 48) — shield-tailed snakes
   Family: Cylindrophiidae (Vol. 48) — pipe snakes
   Family: Aniliidae (Vol. 48) — South American pipe snake
   Family: Xenopeltidae (Vol. 48) — Asian sunbeam snakes
   Family: Loxocemidae (Vol. 48) — American sunbeam snake
   Family: Acrochordidae (Vol. 48) — file snakes
   Family: Boidae (Vol. 48) — boas
   Family: Bolyeriidae (Vol. 48) — Round Island boas
   Family: Tropidophiidae (Vol. 48) — wood snakes
   Family: Pythonidae (Vol. 48) — pythons
   Family: Colubridae (Vol. 49) — colubrids
   Family: Atractaspididae (Vol. 49) — African burrowing snakes
   Family: Elapidae (Vol. 50) — cobras
   Family: Viperidae (Vol. 50) — vipers and pit vipers

ORDER: Testudines (Vol. 47) — turtles, terrapins, and tortoises
ORDER: Crocodylia (Vol. 47) — crocodiles, alligators, and caimans
ORDER: Rhynchocephalia (Vol. 44) — tuataras

may have been described and named at different times without the zoologists realizing it was one species.

Classification allows us to make statements about larger groups of animals. For example, all rattlesnakes are vipers—along with other vipers they are placed in the family Viperidae. All vipers are placed with all other snakes in the suborder Serpentes; snakes are related to lizards, which are in the suborder Sauria, and so these two groups combine to form the order Squamata in the class Reptilia.

An important point must be made about the current scientific knowledge of these animals. New discoveries are being made every day, from the biology of individual creatures to the finding and naming of new species. Our knowledge of the relationships among the different groups is changing constantly. In addition, the number of species known increases all the time, particularly in the light of the very latest DNA analysis techniques that are available to zoologists.

WHAT IS AN AMPHIBIAN?

Amphibians are vertebrates that evolved from fish about 350 to 400 million years ago. They share some characteristics with fish, and most of them return to the water for the most important event in their life—reproduction. All amphibians have certain characteristics in common with each other, including an aquatic larval stage (known as tadpoles), although some do not need water to lay their eggs—instead, they develop inside the egg capsule or, in a few cases, inside the body of one of their parents.

While the body shape of amphibians can vary, they are all covered with skin through which they can breathe. In order to do this, the skin has to be kept moist with secretions produced by glands just below the surface, so many amphibians are slightly moist or slimy to the touch. Most of them live in damp places to avoid drying out. However, some species rely more on skin breathing (cutaneous respiration) than others, and a few can even survive in deserts because they have evolved physical and behavioral adaptations to that hostile environment.

As a very rough guide, amphibians with dry skin, such as typical toads in the genus *Bufo*, tend to use their lungs more and their skin less than those with moist skin, such as most typical frogs in the genus *Rana*. At the opposite extreme a number of amphibians—especially newts and salamanders, but also a few frogs and caecilians—are totally aquatic and never voluntarily leave the water, even after they have transformed into adults.

CLASS AMPHIBIA—3 orders, 44 families, over 5,359 species

Order Gymnophiona—caecilians: 6 families, about 36 genera, 159 species

Order Caudata (Urodela)—salamanders and newts: 10 families, 58 genera, over 400 species

Order Anura—frogs and toads: 28 families, about 346 genera, over 4,800 species

---

Amphibians are divided into three groups, or orders. They are the Caudata (formerly Urodela), which includes the newts and salamanders, the Anura (frogs and toads), and the Gymnophiona (caecilians).

Caecilians

The Gymnophiona contains about 159 species and is not very well known. Its members are elongated amphibians that are mostly restricted to tropical countries. They have a series of annuli, or rings, around their bodies, and they resemble earthworms. Caecilians have internal fertilization; some species lay eggs, but others give birth to live young. Some spend their whole lives in water, whereas others leave the water after they have metamorphosed and live in burrows in damp soil and leaf litter.

Definitions and Exceptions

The word amphibian comes from the Greek *amphi* and *bios*, literally meaning "two lives," and amphibians are often described as vertebrates that have an aquatic larval stage and an adult stage that lives on land. There are many exceptions to that description, however, including some species that do not have an aquatic larval stage as well as others that do not have a terrestrial adult stage.

Nevertheless, all amphibians (with the possible exception of the caecilians) are easily recognizable for what they are: They are animals with smooth, moist skins; they are more or less tied to damp habitats, and they nearly always require a body of fresh water in which to breed.

↑ Likely to be mistaken for large earthworms, caecilians are long-bodied, limbless amphibians with virtually no tail. This is an Asiatic yellow-striped caecilian, Ichthyophis *species*.

→ *Frogs come in many sizes and colors. Some, like Rhacophorus arboreus, the Japanese treefrog, live in trees and build foam nests around their eggs.*

↓ *Typical salamanders have an elongated body, a long tail, and two pairs of legs, as in Rhyacotriton cascadae, the cascade torrent salamander.*

There are many gaps in our knowledge of them because they are so difficult to find and observe, and it is likely that many more species await discovery.

Newts and Salamanders

The other two groups are more familiar. Newts and salamanders, of which there are just over 400 species, typically have roughly cylindrical bodies with a tail and four legs (although some have only two legs). Many of them return to water at some stage, often in the spring, to lay their eggs. Some develop enlarged fins and brighter colors at this time. Others breed on land.

Newts and salamanders are found mostly in the Northern Hemisphere in Europe, Asia, and in North, Central, and South America, but a few species reach extreme northern Africa. They shun the light and live in dark, damp places, rarely appearing on the surface in the daytime except during rain. Some species live in caves, and others live in underground streams; several of them do not metamorphose, living their entire lives as larvae and breeding in that condition.

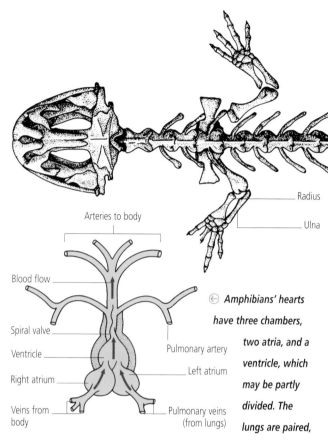

⊕ Fertilized eggs of amphibians have gelatinous envelopes but lack the protective membrane found in all higher vertebrates. Amphibian eggs also lack shells and therefore must be laid in fresh water or in moist places to avoid drying out. Larvae possess external gills, and in frog tadpoles they become enclosed in a chamber by a flap of skin (the operculum). Metamorphosis from larva to adult stage is often abrupt, and the two forms may differ markedly in structure.

Unfertilized egg

Unswollen gelatinous envelope (jelly)

Vitelline membrane

Fertilized egg

Inner jelly capsule

Outer gelatinous envelope (jelly)

Radius

Ulna

Arteries to body

Blood flow

Spiral valve

Ventricle

Right atrium

Veins from body

Pulmonary artery

Left atrium

Pulmonary veins (from lungs)

⊖ Amphibians' hearts have three chambers, two atria, and a ventricle, which may be partly divided. The lungs are paired, but in four families of salamanders they are sometimes reduced or completely absent; in caecilians the left lung is greatly reduced.

Amphibian Fertilization

Fertilization in amphibians can be internal or external. Nearly all frogs have external fertilization: The male fertilizes the eggs by releasing his sperm over them as they emerge from the female's body. This is usually done while he is clasping her in a hold known as "amplexus." Amplexus helps align the male and female cloacae so that the eggs have the best chance of being fertilized.

Most salamanders, however, have internal fertilization: The male's sperm fertilizes the female's eggs while they are still in her body. Internal fertilization is less wasteful than external fertilization, which can be a hit-and-miss affair, with sperm being washed away before it reaches some of the eggs. Internal fertilization also allows salamanders to mate on the land, whereas most frogs have to mate in the water—not always the safest or most convenient place. The only salamanders that have external fertilization are species

that are thought to have evolved early on, many of which live in water, such as the hellbenders. All caecilians have internal fertilization.

With internal fertilization the male deposits a package of sperm (a spermatophore) after courtship that can include amplexus or after a visual display with little or no contact. The female immediately picks up the spermatophore with her cloaca and transfers it to a spermatheca—a small chamber near the end of her reproductive tract. The spermatophore stays there until the eggs move down the oviduct, past the spermatheca, at which point they are fertilized. Some species can store sperm in the spermatheca for many months or even years, while others can store it only for a few days or weeks. In live-bearing species the sperm fertilizes the eggs while they are still high up inside the oviduct, where they continue their development.

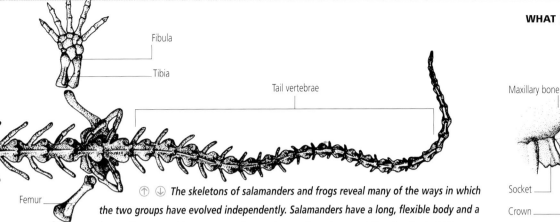

Fibula

Tibia

Tail vertebrae

Maxillary bone

Pedicle

Socket

Crown

Joint

Femur

⊕ ⊕ *The skeletons of salamanders and frogs reveal many of the ways in which the two groups have evolved independently. Salamanders have a long, flexible body and a long tail supported by many vertebrae, whereas frogs have no tail and a short, rigid backbone consisting of a greatly reduced number of vertebrae. The fore- and hind limbs of salamanders are of roughly equal size; but the hind limbs of most frogs have become greatly lengthened, enabling them to leap large distances, and they are supported by a massive, strong pelvic girdle. Frogs have much larger heads relative to their body size, and both groups have very wide mouths, enabling them to take large prey. Their skulls provide plenty of space for their well-developed eyes.*

⊕ *Amphibians have pedicellate teeth, with the crown attached to a narrow pedicel (or base) by uncalcified fibrous tissue, allowing the tooth to bend inward. Salamanders and caecilians have teeth on all jawbones; most frogs lack teeth on the lower jaw, and a few lack teeth on the upper jaw.*

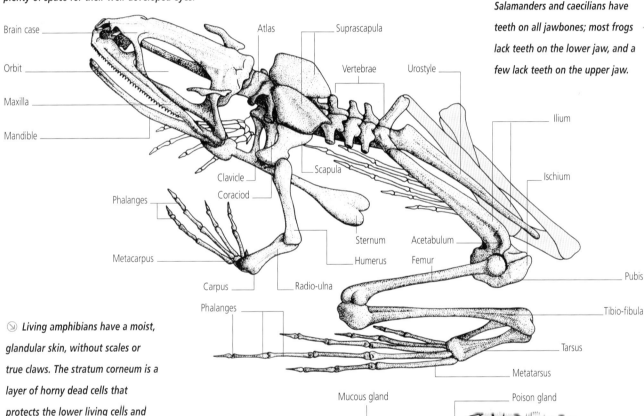

Brain case

Atlas

Suprascapula

Orbit

Vertebrae

Urostyle

Maxilla

Mandible

Ilium

Scapula

Ischium

Phalanges

Clavicle

Coraciod

Metacarpus

Sternum

Acetabulum

Femur

Pubis

Carpus

Radio-ulna

Humerus

Phalanges

Tibio-fibula

Tarsus

Metatarsus

⊘ *Living amphibians have a moist, glandular skin, without scales or true claws. The stratum corneum is a layer of horny dead cells that protects the lower living cells and helps reduce water loss. The dermis is well supplied with blood vessels, which is important since the skin serves as the respiratory organ. Mucous secretions keep the skin moist, allowing respiratory gases to pass in and out of the skin. Poison glands may be grouped together as in the warts of toads.*

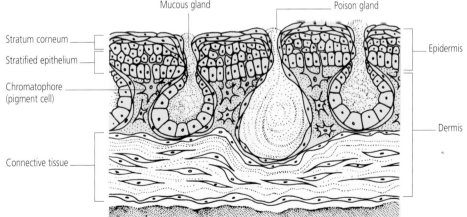

Mucous gland

Poison gland

Stratum corneum

Epidermis

Stratified epithelium

Chromatophore
(pigment cell)

Dermis

Connective tissue

Most newts and salamanders are rather dull in color to match the background against which they live, but several have brightly colored undersides. Others have bold warning colors to signal that they have poison glands in their skin. Many cave-dwelling species are pale, and their internal organs are sometimes visible through their skin.

Adult newts and salamanders eat invertebrates such as earthworms and grubs, and large species may also eat other amphibians and small vertebrates such as mice. Their larvae are carnivorous and eat small aquatic invertebrates such as crustaceans, which are often abundant in the rich waters in which they develop.

Most salamanders have internal fertilization and lay eggs that they attach to stones or water plants. However, a few primitive species have external fertilization. A few

Cutaneous Respiration

Aquatic salamanders, caecilians, and frogs may absorb all (or nearly all) the oxygen they need through their skin. In this way they avoid having to come to the surface to breathe at regular intervals. Members of the salamander family Plethodontidae have done away with lungs altogether and are commonly called lungless salamanders.

Because of the surface-area-to-body-mass ratio most of the "skin breathers" are small; but some larger species also breathe through their skin, using anatomical and behavioral "tricks" to increase the amount of oxygen they can take in.

Aquatic skin breathers need to live in waters that are rich in oxygen, which usually means cool, fast-flowing streams with turbulence. Wide mountain rivers and streams that run over gravel and rocks, forming riffles, are ideal and are the home of species such as the hellbender, *Cryptobranchus alleganiensis*, and aquatic frogs such as the Lake Titicaca frog, *Telmatobius culeus*. These amphibians may enhance their oxygen uptake even more by developing highly vascular skin—frilly folds of skin along their flanks that increase their surface area—or by shaking periodically to prevent oxygen-depleted water from forming a "jacket" around them.

give birth to well-developed larvae, and a couple of species retain the larvae in their oviducts until they are fully developed, at which point they are born on land.

Frogs and Toads

Frogs and toads are the most successful group of amphibians, with about 4,800 species found throughout most of the world except Antarctica. They are most numerous in tropical regions, where over 50 species may live side by side in a small area of forest. They can coexist because they have diversified into many different lifestyles, or "niches." For example, there may be species living in the forest canopy, in tree holes, in leaf litter, or in burrows, all within a small area of forest. There are also variations in body size, in the prey they eat, the methods by which they find it, and their breeding places.

Frogs and toads may be active by day or by night, they may rely on camouflage for defense against predators, or they may be brightly colored to warn of potent toxins in their skin. All these variations limit the amount of competition between species.

Frogs and toads are carnivorous, and their prey includes animals as diverse as small soil-dwelling invertebrates that are almost invisible to the human eye up to mice, rats, and snakes, depending on the size of the frog. Many species also eat smaller frogs and toads, and some eat the young of their own species. They may actively search for prey, or they may wait in ambush for it. Many species' tadpoles, however, are herbivorous, feeding on the layers of algae and bacteria that accumulate on rocks, plants, and other underwater debris. They feed by rasping away at these surfaces, using several rows of teeth positioned above and below the mouth.

Frogs and toads have a remarkably varied repertoire of breeding habits. With just a handful of exceptions they have external fertilization—the male releases sperm over the eggs as the female lays them. Males of most species find mates by calling. Frogs are among the most vocal of animals, with several hundred males sometimes coming together to form breeding choruses that can be heard for several miles. Most North American and European species lay their eggs in ponds and rivers. The eggs hatch into

⊖ *A frog fossil from France,* Rana aquensis, *dates from the Oligocene epoch, beginning 37 million years ago. It is believed that all three groups of modern amphibians shared a common ancestor.*

tadpoles that subsequently develop legs, then lungs, and finally absorb their tails before emerging onto land as small replicas of their parents.

In other parts of the world, however, breeding does not always follow the same pattern. There are species that lay their eggs out of the water, sometimes on leaves overhanging ponds, for example, so that the tadpoles can drip into the water as they hatch. Sometimes they lay their eggs in damp moss, where the whole of their development takes place inside the egg, and they hatch as froglets. In other species the parents carry the eggs, and sometimes also the tadpoles, to protect them during the early part of their development and to ensure that they get a good start.

Amphibian Ancestors

The earliest amphibian fossils have been found in Australia and Greenland. They were formed in the Devonian Period (410 to 325 million years ago), when the continents were joined into a single landmass (known as Pangaea), and Greenland lay over the equator. Most scientists think that amphibians sprang from a group of fish whose members are extinct now. They are known as the crossopterygians, and they had lungs and bony frames to their fins.

⊖ *From fish to amphibian. Crossopterygian fish,* Eusthenopteron *(1);* Ichthyostega, *one of the earliest amphibians, c. 300 million years ago (2).*

⊖ *Giant amphibians from the Triassic, 225–190 million years ago.* Mastodonsaurus *(3) measured 13 feet (4 m) from snout to tip of tail;* Diadectes *(4) was 10 feet (3 m) long; and* Eryops *(5) was smaller, at 5 feet (1.5 m) in length.*

The fins evolved eventually into four limbs, allowing the early ancestors of amphibians to crawl out of the water and support themselves on the land. The reason they left the water is anybody's guess, but it may have been to avoid competition, find new sources of food, or colonize new bodies of water when their pools started to dry out or became too crowded. Most of these early amphibians had already died out by the Jurassic Period, 220 million years ago.

The origins of the three living orders of amphibians and their relationships to each other are a mystery. The oldest fossil amphibian to bear any resemblance to species alive today was a primitive frog called *Triadobatrachus* that lived about 250 million years ago. It had more vertebrae than modern frogs and a short tail. Fossil salamanders have also been found, including one from China dating from about 150 million years ago. It differs little from the surviving species of hellbenders and giant salamanders. There are no fossils showing the links between the fishlike ancestors and modern salamanders and caecilians. This gives us no clue to the appearance of the ancestors of either of these groups or to when they may have started to follow different evolutionary paths. We will have to wait until older fossil amphibians are discovered before we can fill in some of the gaps.

Conservation

Reading about amphibians and their problems in a modern world can be a sobering and, at times, depressing experience. Time and time again the phrases "diminishing populations," "threatened with extinction," and "possibly extinct" crop up.

Species at risk range from the frail-looking olm, *Proteus anguinus*, in Italy and Slovenia (whose cave-system habitat is being slowly poisoned by chemicals seeping down through the limestone) to the pugnacious and seemingly indestructible giant salamanders of the Pacific Northwest, whose crystal-clear mountain streams

⊖ *Now probably extinct, the Costa Rican golden toad,* Bufo periglenes, *was discovered in the 1960s. Over 1,000 were seen at a breeding site in 1987; but only 11 were present in 1990, and none have been seen since.*

are becoming silted up through clear-cutting of forests. This causes silt to accumulate on the riverbeds, filling in the spaces between the gravel in which the larvae live, clogging up their gills, and making it difficult for them to find food. The unique and rare tailed frog, *Ascaphus truei*, which lives in these streams, is also facing an uncertain future.

Problems exist on a small scale at a local level and on a large scale globally. Local pressures include deforestation in rain forests and elsewhere, draining of wetlands, and small-scale pollution such as runoff from paved roads and dumping of chemicals in ponds and streams. Many small farm and village ponds used for breeding by countless generations of newts, salamanders, frogs, and toads have been filled in for safety reasons or for convenience. They are often replaced by a galvanized trough and a hose pipe or are filled with supermarket shopping trolleys and other detritus. Even species that were common until recently have started to disappear from the countryside at an alarming rate.

On a global level conservationists have identified several other causes for declining populations. They include the depletion of ozone in the atmosphere, which may increase exposure to ultraviolet (UVB)

radiation, possibly affecting eggs and developing larvae; the accumulation of pollutants, including acid rain, in the atmosphere and water systems; changes in weather patterns; and viral and other diseases. The latter may be aggravated by stress caused by other factors and may also be spread by the movement and introduction of exotic species, so it is often difficult to separate the different causes in any particular case.

Driven to Extinction

One of the more worrying aspects is the decline of species that has taken place in some of the most pristine habitats on earth, including nature reserves and national parks. Herpetologists have monitored amphibian populations in several parts of the world since the 1980s, and in 1991 the Declining Amphibian Population Task Force (DAPTF) was established to coordinate research throughout the world. Some of the findings include 36 species that are thought to have gone extinct recently, three of which disappeared before they were even named.

⊕ *In Europe signs warn motorists of the seasonal presence of frogs and toads. Other measures are being taken to conserve local toad populations: A female toad carrying a male approaches a wide-gauge grid. They will fall through and continue their journey safely under the road.*

Amazing Statistics

The largest living amphibian is the Chinese giant salamander, *Andrias davidianus*, which can reach almost 6 feet (1.8 m) in length and weigh up to 50 pounds (22 kg). The largest frog is the Goliath frog, *Conraua goliath* from West Africa, one of which measured 34.5 inches (88 cm) and weighed just over 8 pounds (3.6 kg). The largest caecilian is *Caecilia thompsoni* (it has no common name), which grows to 5 feet (1.5 m).

Establishing the smallest species is harder. Since they all start life small, it can be difficult to know if you are measuring an adult or juvenile. The smallest caecilian is probably *Grandisonia brevis* from the Seychelles, which has a maximum size of about 4.4 inches (11 cm), and the smallest salamander is *Thorius arboreus*, one of the lungless salamanders from the highlands of Mexico.

There are several contenders for the smallest frog species, including several rain frogs in the genus *Eleutherodactylus*, a saddle-back toad, *Psyllophryne didactyla* from southern Brazil, and the stump-toed frog, *Stumpffia tridactyla* from Madagascar. They all grow to about 0.4 inches (10 mm) in length.

Many amphibians have natural life spans of one year or less, but others are more long-lived. The record is held by a Japanese giant salamander, *Andrias japonicus*, which lived 55 years in captivity, while a fire salamander, *Salamandra salamandra*, lived 50 years, and a European common toad, *Bufo bufo*, lived to the age of 36.

→ *In southern Cameroon a boy holds up a Goliath frog,* Conraua goliath. *These giants of the frog world can reach 34.5 inches (88 cm) in size and weigh as much as a domestic cat.*

Eleven of the extinct species are small *Atelopus* toads from the Andes of Ecuador, which (superficially at least) is one the least changed habitats in the world. In addition, another 26 species of frogs and toads have not been seen for five years or more and may well be extinct, and another 91 are Critically Endangered (IUCN).

These figures come from a small number of countries, among which Venezuela, Ecuador, Brazil, and Australia figure prominently. The situation in Central and West Africa, for instance, or in parts of Southeast Asia has not even been studied thoroughly. Secretive species such as many frogs, toads, and salamanders, and all the caecilians, are so poorly understood that they could go extinct before we even know of their existence.

Why should we care? From a purely selfish point of view we should consider that amphibians are indicators of the health of our environment. Because of their need for aquatic as well as terrestrial habitats, and because they respire across the surface of their necessarily delicate skin, amphibians react more quickly than most other animals to factors that affect their environments.

But what affects their health today may well affect ours tomorrow. Setting that fact aside, the disappearance of even one species affects anyone who values biodiversity. Frogs, newts, and salamanders are part of the web of life that makes nature so interesting and important to everyone. Some of them are attractive, many have interesting stories to tell, and all deserve their place in the world. The American environmentalist Aldo Leopold summed it up when he said, "The art of intelligent tinkering is to keep all the parts."

Amphibians as Pets

Generally speaking, amphibians are slightly more difficult to keep in captivity than reptiles because they tend to be more sensitive to environmental conditions. Because they breathe through their permeable skins, they also take up toxins that way, so they must have spotlessly clean accommodation and water that is free from chemical contaminants, including disinfectants and cleaning materials. It is a good idea to choose captive-bred specimens whenever possible because they will adapt better than wild ones, and keeping them will not contribute to the decline of wild stocks.

Aquatic species are often the easiest option because there is plenty of equipment for keeping aquarium fish that is equally suitable for species such as clawed frogs, dwarf aquarium frogs, and axolotls. The first two species are tropical, but the axolotl does not require heated water, just good filtration. Other species, such as newts, spend part of each year in the water and may refuse to feed unless they are given access to it. Several others are flexible and can be kept in water or on the land. The oriental fire-bellied toad, *Bombina orientalis*, is one of the most popular pet species and requires a setup that is roughly half land and half water. Other popular species are the horned frogs, *Ceratophrys*, which can be kept in shallow water or on a moist substrate such as moss.

Salamanders and most frogs and toads are terrestrial for almost the whole year, only needing water for a short period for breeding. Unless you are hoping to breed these species, they can be kept in a terrestrial setup all year round, with a layer of leaf litter and places to hide, such as pieces of flat stone or bark. Attractive vivaria can be built using living plants and even running water; but that is rarely necessary except in the case of certain difficult tropical species, such as poison dart frogs, which beginners should avoid.

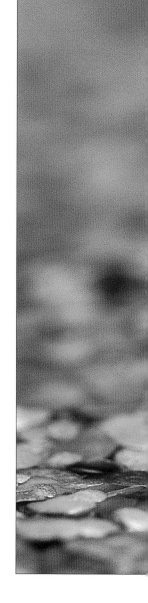

A rain-forest environment has been carefully created in a terrarium at a Dutch zoo. The tank is home to a number of poison dart frogs, which are highly toxic and best left to expert keepers.

Creating the Right Conditions

Many amphibians, even those from the tropics, prefer cooler temperatures than reptiles, and heating is often necessary only in a very cold climate. There are exceptions, however, and advice should be sought from a specialized publication or the place where the amphibians were bought. Similarly, light should be subdued because amphibians lead secretive lives, and they become stressed if they are forced to live under the glare of bright lights.

Humidity is obviously important, and even terrestrial species such as the toads, *Bufo*, should have their cage sprayed with water regularly to make sure they do not dry out. Ventilation is equally important, since amphibians do not thrive in a stagnant atmosphere.

Nearly all amphibians are insectivorous: Even large species, such as the horned frogs (which will eat small mammals and other frogs), can live their entire lives on a diet of insects such as crickets and locusts. Many species (including aquatic frogs and newts) also like worms, which can be obtained (or dug up) in a variety of sizes. Most frog and toad tadpoles are herbivorous and will usually feed on algae that builds up on the surface of plants and rocks, but they will also eat flaked fish food and a variety of other special diets.

Encouraging Amphibians

It is possible to enjoy amphibians without having to keep them captive. A small garden pond with an overgrown area around the edge can provide an ideal habitat for many species of frogs, toads, newts, and salamanders,

⬆ *The oriental fire-bellied toad,* Bombina orientalis, *is probably the best terrestrial frog for the beginner to keep as a pet. It is named for its attractive underside, which is orange with black spots.*

and will help replace habitats that have been lost through urban development. Some amphibians will visit the pond to breed in the spring and then disappear into the surrounding countryside; but others will remain close by, especially if there are hiding places in the form of log piles and rockeries. Artificial substances, such as weed killers or pesticides, should be avoided. If all goes well, the garden should not need pesticides, since the amphibians will keep pests under control. Be aware that in many places it is illegal to introduce nonlocal species; however, even a small pond that provides a home to a single species of frog or newt can be very rewarding.

CAECILIANS

Caecilians (the word is pronounced in nearly the same way as "Sicilians") are elongated, wormlike burrowing amphibians that live only in the tropics. They are found in Central and South America, Central Africa, the Seychelles, India, Sri Lanka, and Southeast Asia. They are absent from North America, Madagascar, and Australasia. Perhaps the most disproportionate distribution is that of the seven endemic species on the tiny Seychelles Islands surrounded by the Indian Ocean. Altogether, there are about 159 species divided among about 36 genera and placed in six families. They form the order Gymnophiona, although they are sometimes wrongly called the Apoda. Hardly any of them have common names.

Caecilians are probably the least-known vertebrates in the world, and their obscurity is rivaled only by another group of wormlike burrowing animals, the worm lizards, or amphisbaenians. Many species of caecilians are represented by only a single specimen in a museum. As a group they have a number of unusual characteristics both in their structure and the way they behave.

Burrowing Characteristics

Caecilians have no limbs or limb girdles, and their heads are very sturdy and bony. Some species have short tails, but most have no tail. The head slopes sharply down to the snout, so that when seen from the side, it is wedge shaped and comes to a point, and when seen from above, it is rounded. The lower jaw is underslung, or countersunk. All these features are associated with a burrowing lifestyle. Their bodies have a series of rings (annuli), each of which corresponds with a vertebra. The rings are separated by grooves. In some species there are additional rings between the primary ones, and in a few there are more between the secondary rings (so there can be one, two, or four rings for each vertebra).

The skin is tough on the outside, but the inner layers have slime glands and poison glands: Caecilians are

The Blue-Ringed Caecilian

Siphonops annulatus is one of the most distinctive caecilians. It is deep blue in color with narrow white rings around its body. The striking coloration may act as a deterrent to predators. It occurs over a wide area in South America, together with four other closely related species in the same genus. Juveniles have never been found, and its natural history is poorly known; but most specimens are collected inside termite nests or in the ground very close to them. Other specimens have been found under garbage on the edges of villages.

⊝ *The rich blue-and-white coloring of* Siphonops annulatus, *the blue-ringed caecilian, may be a clue to the fact that toxins have been discovered in its skin and may deter predators.*

distasteful, or even toxic, to many predators. In South America, however, coral snakes, *Micrurus*, often prey on them. In some species the inner layers of skin in the region of the grooves contain rows or patches of small, bony scales. They are like fish scales rather than reptile scales. Primitive caecilians (those that evolved early on) have groups of scales along the length of the body, others have them only in grooves toward the rear of the body, while the most advanced species have no scales.

A Range of Colors

The skin also contains the pigment cells that give the animals their color. Most species are dull gray, bluish, or black, but some are more colorful. *Siphonops annulatus* is blue with thin white lines that coincide with the annular grooves, and *Microcaecilia albiceps* from the Amazon Basin is bluish gray with a white or pale-pink head. Several species, such as *Boulengerula boulengeri* from Tanzania and *Schistometopum thomense* from West Africa, are yellow or orange, perhaps to warn of toxic substances in their skin. Some of the *Ichthyophis* species from South and Southeast Asia are dark brown or black along their backs and yellow underneath. The Koh Tao caecilian, *Ichthyophis kohtaoensis* from Thailand, which is sometimes imported through the pet trade, starts life as a uniform brown juvenile and acquires a bright yellow stripe down its side as it grows.

Sensory Tentacles

Caecilians have a unique sense organ in the form of a tentacle on each side of the head between the eye and the nostril. This organ detects chemicals (so it is basically an organ of smell). When in use, each tentacle is visible as a small pimple, but it is longer than it looks because the base of the tentacle sits in a sheath that remains hidden beneath the surface. When the caecilian withdraws its tentacles, it closes the openings through which they protruded. It can extend the tentacles by using pressure from fluids secreted by the orbital gland (the gland that keeps the eye moist in other vertebrates). Molecules collected by the tentacles are sent to the Jacobson's organ, which is next to the olfactory part of the brain. Bearing in mind that caecilians must close their nostrils when they are burrowing to prevent them from getting clogged with soil, the tentacles probably help them detect food items.

Members of the family Scolecomorphidae have their tentacles positioned on the underside of the snout in front of their underslung mouth. Their vestigial eyes have also migrated to this position and are located at the base of the tentacles. When the animal extends its tentacles, the eyes go with them, carried outside its skull, up the stalk, and onto the tips of the tentacles.

In most species of caecilians, however, the eyes are vestigial (reduced) and covered by skin, bone, or both. They can sometimes be seen as small dark or light areas depending on the animal's pigmentation. Despite the primitive design of the eyes, they have retinas and lenses, and are sensitive to changes in light intensity. Their ears have no external openings; but one ear bone is still present, and it connects with a bone in the lower jaw, allowing the animal to detect low-frequency vibrations.

Respiration

With one possible exception caecilians have lungs, but the arrangement varies according to species. Most terrestrial species have large right lungs (up to 75 percent of their body length) and small left lungs (less than 10 percent of their body length). *Boulengerula taitanus* from Kenya apparently has no left lung at all, and *Hypogeophis rostratus* from the Seychelles has only a rudimentary left lung. Aquatic species have two large lungs, possibly used for buoyancy as well as respiration. One caecilian that was collected in the 18th century from South America appears to have no lungs, but whether or not that is true will remain a mystery until additional specimens come to light. All species of caecilians can also breathe through their skin and through the lining of their mouth.

Locomotion

Although they are thoroughly burrowing animals, caecilians are sometimes washed out of their burrows, during heavy rain, for example. On the surface they use a type of locomotion similar to snakes and other legless vertebrates, moving by bending their bodies from side to side and pushing against irregularities. Aquatic caecilians use the same form of movement to swim through water. When they are burrowing in soil, caecilians travel in a straight line, using their wedge-shaped, strongly reinforced skull as a ram to push through the earth. At the same time, the muscles that surround their vertebrae contract and expand, decreasing and increasing the diameter of their body in different places. Where the

⊖ *Earthworms form the major part of the diet of most caecilians, as in* Caecilia tentaculata *from Guyana. Caecilians may be preyed on in turn by other amphibians, such as toads.*

diameter increases, the animal jams itself into the burrow and provides purchase for other sections to move forward. These sections expand in turn, allowing other sections to move forward, so there is a sequence of rippling "push-and-pull" cycles running along the body.

Feeding

Because of their shape caecilians are restricted to eating elongated prey. Also, because they live under the ground, they are restricted largely to prey that can be found there. Earthworms form the bulk of the diet of the few species that have been studied. Caecilians also eat earthworms in captivity; but some of the larger species will tackle larger prey such as lizards and small rodents, and aquatic caecilians will eat dead fish.

Capturing prey is a simple matter of approaching it and grasping it in the jaws. The jaws open in an unusual way: The lower jaw stays more or less stationary, and the upper jaw opens upward (rather like a crocodile's). This is probably an adaptation to feeding in the confined space of a burrow. The teeth are well developed on both jaws; they curve backward for holding slippery prey and have sharp edges for cutting. As they chew, the backward curve of the teeth allows the prey to move down the caecilian's throat.

Reproduction

For a small group of animals caecilians have very diverse life cycles. Courtship has not been seen in any terrestrial species, but fertilization is internal. Male caecilians have a protrusible organ, the phalodeum. It is formed from the lining of the rear part of the cloaca and is inserted into the female's vent in order to deliver the spermatophore directly into her reproductive tract. The female may lay her eggs in burrows near the edges of streams. She coils around the eggs until they hatch into gilled larvae that wriggle down into the water, where they metamorphose into small adults and crawl back to the land. Other species skip the larval stage: The female lays her eggs on

Caecilians of the Seychelles

Seven species of caecilians live on the Seychelles. The 41 granite islands came into being when the ancient supercontinent of Pangaea broke up, by which time caecilians of some sort must have been present already. They are distributed on several islands, but they are restricted to damp areas, and some are becoming rare. Drainage of lowland marshes on Frégate Island for tourism purposes has affected the ranges of two species. One, *Grandisonia alternans*, may be extinct on that island because its aquatic larvae require standing water. The other species, *Hypogeophis rostratus*, has direct development and is more resilient, but by a bizarre twist large numbers seem to have been killed by the endangered Seychelles magpie robins, *Copsychus sechellarum*. Populations of the birds have grown since BirdLife International began to provide food for them in 1989, and now there are more on the island than ever before. Signs of pecking on dead caecilians point to mutilation by the birds, although they appear not to eat them. Other predators include introduced pigs and chickens.

Hypogeophis rostratus grows to 14 inches (36 cm). It is common on the Seychelles, but the long-term impact on numbers due to killing by magpie robins is not known.

land and coils around them until they hatch into small adult replicas.

Members of other species bear live young. Females retain the developing eggs in their oviducts, where, after absorbing the yolk sacs, they feed on a secretion from the oviduct wall. They scrape off this "uterine milk" using special teeth that they lose when they grow adult teeth. While they are developing, the embryos (usually between two and 25 in number) obtain oxygen and possibly nourishment from the mother's bloodstream via a pair of large fetal gills. The gills are well supplied with capillaries and are shed just before the young caecilians are born, or in the case of some aquatic species, a few hours after birth. The mother apparently eats the discarded gills. Gestation lasts seven to 11 months, during which time the embryos grow significantly, requiring a substantial reproductive effort from the female.

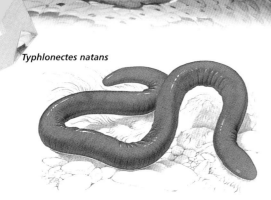
Typhlonectes natans

Common name Aquatic caecilians (rubber eels, black eels, Sicilian eels, rubber caecilians)

Scientific name *Typhlonectes* sp.

Family Typhlonectidae (sometimes regarded as a subfamily—Typhlonectinae—of the Caeciliidae)

Order Gymnophiona

Number of species 3

Size 18 in (46 cm) to 22 in (56 cm)

Key features The 3 species are all very similar and almost featureless; long and slender with a smooth, slimy, rubbery skin; eyes very small and barely discernible; no tail; gray or blue-gray in color without markings; similar to an eel but without fins

Habits Completely aquatic and active mostly at night, hiding by day in a burrow or among aquatic vegetation

Breeding Live-bearers with small numbers of young (up to 9); gestation period 215–225 days

Diet Aquatic invertebrates and slow-moving vertebrates; may also scavenge dead animals

Habitat Poorly known but thought to be slow-moving rivers, lakes, and swamps

Distribution Northern South America

Status Probably common

Similar species None, but can be mistaken for eels

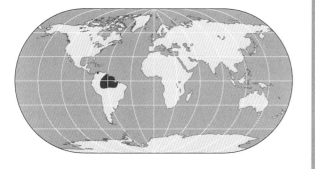

South American Aquatic Caecilians

Typhlonectes sp.

The fully aquatic caecilians come from South America. They are probably the most familiar caecilians and are often sold in pet stores under the name of "rubber eels."

THE THREE SPECIES OF South American aquatic caecilians are almost indistinguishable from each other. Known sometimes as rubber eels in the pet trade, they are thought of by most dealers as fish and sold as such.

Typhlonectes species are completely aquatic, never voluntarily leaving the water. They live in muddy rivers, swamps, and lakes, apparently hiding in mud burrows and emerging to feed at night. In the colored water in which they live, their lack of eyes is of no importance, and they use their sense of smell to find food. They have the same chemosensory tentacles as other caecilians, but they are unable to protrude and retract them.

Typhlonectes and Their Relatives

The aquatic caecilians belong to the family Typhlonectidae, all of which live in South America. There are 4 genera and 13 species altogether in the family.

Family Typhlonectidae:
Genus *Chthonerpeton*—8 species from Argentina, Brazil, Ecuador, and Uruguay
Genus *Nectocaecilia*—1 species from the Upper Amazon, *N. petersii*
Genus *Potomotyphlus*—1 species from the Amazon Basin, *P. kaupii*
Genus *Typhlonectes*—3 species, *T. compressicauda* from the eastern coast of Brazil to the eastern slopes of Peru and north to Guyana; *T. cunhai*, known only from Manaus, Brazil; *T. natans* from northern Colombia and northwest Venezuela

↑ *Typhlonectes natans is native to Colombia. Its rubbery body is dark gray or lavender in color, and it swims using wavelike movements.*

and female remain joined for at least three hours. The gestation period is between 215 and 225 days, after which the female gives birth to up to nine young. They measure about 6 inches (15 cm) at birth—almost 40 percent of the mother's length. Their length will have increased sixfold since absorbing their yolk, due to nourishment obtained in the uterus (uterine milk). There is also evidence that they consume part of the uterine wall as they develop. They shed their enormous external gills within a few hours of birth, and metamorphosis takes the form of thickening of the skin, development of the tentacles, and replacement of the fetal teeth by adult teeth shortly after birth. They feed on small versions of the same food as the adults, growing quickly and shedding their skin at frequent intervals. As adults they will continue to shed their skin every week or two.

One species observed in an aquarium appeared to be incapable of locating food by sight, but its sense of smell was clearly acute—it detected an earthworm dropped into the water within seconds. In addition to eating living organisms, *Typhlonectes* are scavengers, feeding on dead fish and other animals.

"His and Hers" Tails
Mating behavior has occurred in aquariums, and all observations are made from captives. Males and females differ from each other in the shape of their "tails" (which are not tails, in fact, but the ends of their bodies). Adult males have rounded ends to their tails, whereas those of females and juveniles are slightly pointed when seen from above. Males are territorial and aggressive toward one another, but females are more peaceful. During mating, which probably takes place at any time of the year, the male

Conservation
The export of these species by fish dealers from Colombia was stopped once the authorities realized they were not fish. However, they are not rare amphibians, and they are among the few that have probably benefitted from human activities, with high densities living near fishing villages and eating the entrails of fish cleaned at the riverside. They are often caught accidentally in seine nets, but collecting for any purpose is unlikely to have a serious effect on their numbers. (A seine net is a long, narrow net laid in a semicircle from a boat and then pulled in from the shore by drawing in each end of the net.) Habitat degradation through pollution is probably the greatest threat to aquatic caecilians, but they appear to be very tolerant of poor water quality.

SALAMANDERS

Salamanders and newts usually have four limbs and a tail, although the sirens have only two limbs, and the amphiumas have four tiny limbs that seem to have little or no function.

There are just over 400 species of newts and salamanders divided into 10 families. Most live in the Northern Hemisphere, especially North America, Europe, and Central Asia. There are no salamanders in Africa south of the Sahara, in Southeast Asia, or in Australia, but there are many species of small, nimble, neotropical salamanders in Central and South America.

Salamanders' lifestyles and characteristics are varied. Some are completely aquatic, and some live in underground streams. Some have no pigment, and some do not metamorphose. Most salamanders, however, live secretive lives in damp places on land. A few climb trees.

Respiration

As in other amphibians, salamanders breathe through the skin as well as the lungs, and some species rely more heavily on their skin for respiration than others. Newts and salamanders, whether in water or on land, usually raise and lower their throat in a rhythmic pumping action. This may serve primarily to shunt air in and out of their lungs, but some gaseous exchange also takes place across the lining of the mouth. At the same time, they are sampling the air for scent molecules that may provide them with information about potential food, predators, mates, rivals, or migratory "landmarks." In many species the sense of smell is more important than sight.

Food and Feeding

All salamanders and newts are carnivorous, and most of their food consists of living animals. A few will learn to

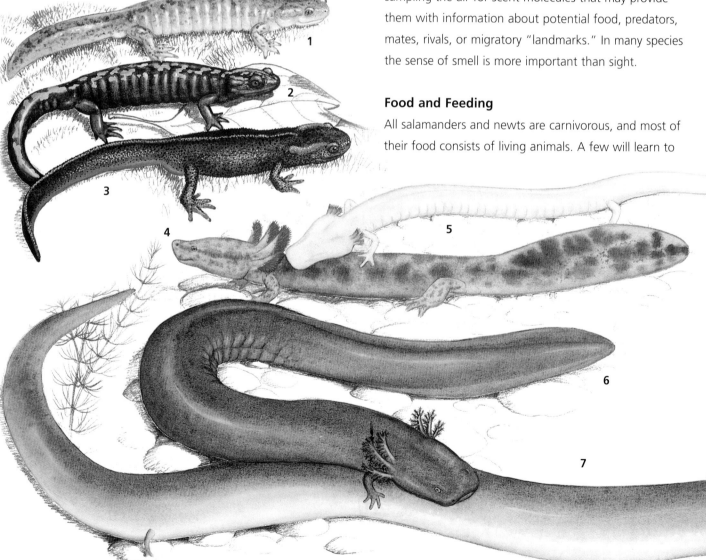

Temperature and Sex

Temperature-dependent sex determination (TDSD) is well known in some reptiles, including turtles, crocodilians, and some lizards, but has rarely been studied in amphibians. Because the sharp-ribbed newt, *Pleurodeles waltl*, has been widely studied and bred in laboratories in large numbers, some interesting facts have come to light. If the eggs are incubated at between 61 and 75°F (16–24°C), a normal 50:50 sex split results. Temperatures higher than that result in more males and also produce some animals that have characteristics of both sexes. In the only related species, the North African sharp-ribbed newt, *P. poireti*, abnormally high temperatures have the reverse effect—they produce more females. Future studies may reveal that TDSD is present in other species.

---

eat stationary objects such as pond pellets, especially if they smell like food; but it is usually movement that attracts their attention. The type of prey is limited by its size and how frequently the salamanders encounter it. Surveys have shown that salamanders and their larvae feed most heavily on whatever is most common.

Food items range enormously in size: Newly hatched salamander larvae prey on aquatic invertebrates so small that they are almost invisible to the human eye, while some of the larger terrestrial species will eat vertebrates such as lizards, frogs, and small rodents. Many salamanders prey heavily on smaller salamander species, and a significant number are cannibalistic.

Aquatic species usually feed by opening their mouth quickly so that water rushes in, bringing the prey animal with it. Terrestrial species either stalk their prey patiently, snapping it up with a final lunge, or capture it with the sticky tip of a protrusible tongue. In some species, such as the cave salamanders (*Speleomantes* species and others), the tongue can reach to a distance approaching their own body length.

Reproduction

Despite the common perception that newts and salamanders migrate to ponds in order to breed every year and then hatch into aquatic larvae before metamorphosing into terrestrial adults, only about one-quarter of known species follow this sequence. Many species are totally aquatic throughout their lives, so migration to breed on land is unnecessary. However, some, such as the hellbenders, migrate upstream and downstream to form aggregations in places that are especially favorable for egg laying. Many other species, including the huge genus of miniature salamanders,

⊙ *Representative species of 5 families of salamanders and newts.*
Hynobiidae: Batrachuperus pinchonii (1), Onychodactylus japonicus (2);
Salamandridae:
Tylototriton taliangensis
(3); Proteidae: mudpuppy,
Necturus maculosus (4); olm,
Proteus anguinus (5); Sirenidae: Siren
lacertina (6); Amphiumidae: Amphiuma means (7).

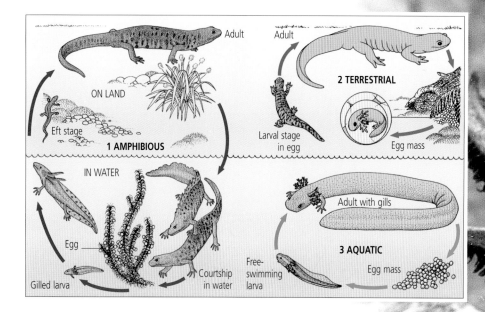

ⓣ *A comparison of the life cycles of salamanders and newts. Many salamanders are completely terrestrial, while newts return to water each year to breed. The axolotl,* Ambystoma mexicanum, *is totally aquatic.*

Bolitoglossa, lay their eggs on land in damp places such as moss or leaf litter, where they develop into fully formed young. Females of many species of salamanders remain with their eggs until they hatch into either aquatic larvae or fully formed young. A few species, such as the alpine salamander, *Salamandra atra*, hold the developing eggs in their oviducts and give birth either to well-developed larvae or to fully developed young.

Growth and development in larval and adult salamanders is marked by periodic skin shedding. The animal often eats its shed skin as it peels away, but the empty, diaphanous skin of a newt can sometimes be found in ponds.

Pedomorphosis, Pedogenesis, and Neoteny

When animals fail to grow up and retain juvenile characteristics throughout their lives, they are said to be pedomorphic (literally "juvenile shaped"). In salamanders the condition involves keeping their external gills, the fins along their bodies, and failing to develop eyelids.

There are two different forms of pedomorphosis. In the first, known as pedogenesis, the animal is genetically programmed to stay as a larva for the whole of its life

ⓣ *A North American blotched tiger salamander larva,* Ambystoma tigrinum melanostictum. *Adults are olive-green in color with black blotches that often form a netlike pattern on the back. The larva is of the pond type.*

and can never change. The other form occurs when pedomorphosis is caused by the environment and is called neoteny. Neotenic larvae can metamorphose if their circumstances change, at least in theory. For instance, if the pond in which they are living dries up, the larvae will metamorphose into adults and move to another pond to avoid dying.

Some pedogenetic salamanders have evolved because they live in environments where changing into adults is not an option. Many of them live in underground rivers and streams. They are better off staying in the water and feeding on other cave-dwelling invertebrates such as shrimp than moving to the land. They include the

Salamander Larvae

Salamander larvae fall into two broad categories. Pond-type larvae have high tail fins and a dorsal fin that reaches almost to their head. During their early stages they have a small structure called a balancer on each side of the head and long, frilly external gills. Their front limbs are only partially developed, and they have no back limbs at all—they develop later. Mole salamanders, European salamanders, and most newts have larvae of the pond type.

Stream-type larvae have a more flattened body. Their fins are narrow, and the dorsal fin only reaches to the base of the tail. They lack balancers, but their back legs are developed and functional as soon as they hatch. These features are all adaptations to living in fast-flowing, clear water containing plenty of oxygen. Examples include the larvae of brook salamanders, torrent salamanders, and many lungless salamanders.

Some scientists recognize a third group, the brook type, which is even more highly adapted for living in flowing water, and they include the torrent salamanders in this group.

The larva of the smooth newt, Triturus vulgaris *from Europe. Typical of the pond-type larva, it has high tail fins and a dorsal fin that almost reaches its head.*

blind cave salamanders, *Eurycea* species, from Texas and Georgia. Both species belong to a family (Plethodontidae) that also contains salamanders with normal life cycles. Others are pedogenetic because they come from ancient families whose members are all totally aquatic. They include the mudpuppies (Proteidae) and the sirens (Sirenidae).

Neotenic salamanders have the best of both worlds. They can live in ponds and streams if they are the best places for them, either because there is plenty of food,

there are fewer predators, or simply because there are fewer hiding places on the land. If their environment changes and being aquatic becomes a drawback, they can transform themselves into land-dwelling adults.

Sometimes a single species of salamander can have two kinds of larvae—those that normally transform into adults and those that transform only if the situation is suitable. A number of the mole salamanders in the family Ambystomatidae fit that category. The family also contains the most famous of all neotenic salamanders, the axolotl, or Mexican mole salamander, *Ambystoma mexicanum*. Some scientists argue that since the salamander never metamorphoses under natural circumstances, it should be termed pedogenetic, but it is easier to think of it as neotenic along with the other members of its family that show this trait.

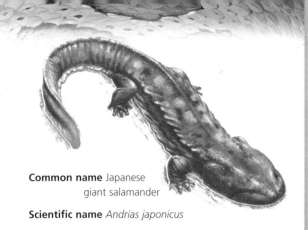

Common name Japanese
giant salamander

Scientific name *Andrias japonicus*

Family Cryptobranchidae

Order Caudata (Urodela)

Size 28 in (71 cm) to 39 in (100 cm); exceptionally to 4.6 ft (1.4 m)

Key features Massive salamander with a flattened head and body; eyes tiny with no lids; limbs short and flattened; tail short and oar shaped with high dorsal and ventral fins; rough skin is reddish brown in color with many folds and wrinkles

Habits Aquatic; nocturnal, hiding by day in burrows or rocky crevices

Breeding Female lays 400–600 eggs, which are guarded by a male until they hatch 6 or 7 weeks later

Diet Aquatic vertebrates and invertebrates

Habitat Wide mountain rivers with rocky or gravelly bottoms

Distribution Japan (southwestern Honshu and Kyushu)

Status Vulnerable (IUCN); affected by habitat destruction and pollution of streams

Similar species The Chinese giant salamander, *Andrias davidianus*, is similar but differs in the pattern of tubercles on its head and throat, and it grows slightly larger than the Japanese species

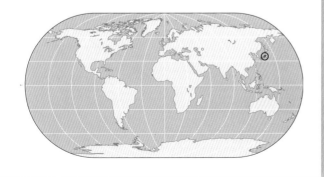

Japanese Giant Salamander
Andrias japonicus

The two species of giant salamanders are the largest living amphibians, measuring up to 39 inches (100 cm) in length and weighing 12 pounds (5 kg) or more. The Japanese species has been declared a national treasure in its homeland.

THE JAPANESE GIANT SALAMANDER is not an attractive animal. It is an important one, however, due to its size and its primitive origins. It is massively built—its body and head are wide and flat. Its short limbs are also flattened from side to side.

Like its close relative the hellbender, *Cryptobranchus alleganiensis*, it can only live in mountain rivers and streams with a high oxygen content and no pollution, and at an altitude of 1,000 to 3,000 feet (300–900 m). The rivers are typically 50 to 60 feet (15–18 m) wide and are shallow, with water flowing over beds that have rocks of varying sizes. There is a good mix of spaces between the rocks, where the larvae live. Adults live in rocky crevices or in burrows at the river edges. They spend their entire lives in the water, but they may venture out during rain. They are active mainly at night and feed on freshwater crustaceans such as crayfish and crabs, as well as fish and amphibians.

ⓘ *The Chinese giant salamander,* Andrias davidianus, *is a close relative of the Japanese giant salamander and is very similar in appearance. It is found in the north, central, south, and southwestern regions of China.*

Underwater Burrows

Their breeding system seems to be similar to that of the hellbender but is not as well documented. They breed in the fall (late August to early September). Males and females travel 100 to 2,000 feet (30–610 m) to good nesting sites. They construct underwater burrows that extend 39 to 60 inches (100–150 cm) into the riverbank and have a single entrance. Large males, called "den masters," can monopolize more than one nest, guarding each one against other males and attacking if necessary. Ripe females enter the nests and lay 400 to 600

eggs in two long strings. The male immediately fertilizes the eggs by releasing sperm over them. They take about two months to hatch, and the larvae are just over 1 inch (3 cm) at hatching. They lose their external gills at three years old, when they measure about 8 inches (20 cm). They take at least five years to reach sexual maturity at about 12 inches (30 cm) for males and 16 inches (41 cm) for females. They can live for at least 50 years in captivity—their natural lifespan is unknown but may be 80 to 90 years. Adult Japanese giant salamanders have few predators other than humans.

Species under Threat

The biggest threat to their survival is pollution of the rivers in which they live. The species has already disappeared from several river systems, and its range has become fragmented as a result. Dams prevent migration up- and downstream. Small populations are therefore vulnerable and cannot recruit from neighboring systems. In the past humans caught them for food (a fate that still applies to the Chinese species, *A. davidianus*), and the eggs were also eaten, especially by pregnant women.

Since the species was declared a national treasure, people in the area where they occur take pride in the salamanders and try to protect

The Chinese Giant Salamander

The Chinese giant salamander, *Andrias davidianus*, is a relative of the Japanese giant salamander. It has a wide range over much of the south of the country and is, if anything, slightly larger than the Japanese species. Its numbers are also declining because its range has been reduced by river pollution and by hunting for human consumption, which still goes on. The average size of captured individuals is declining, indicating that most of the large ones (the prime breeding stock) have already been taken. Because it is a culinary delicacy, the salamander is bred in captivity, and farms have been established in several provinces. They have been a partial success and may be the best hope for the survival of the species.

their habitat. Attempts to provide them with artificial nest sites in the form of buried pipes, however, have met with only partial success—females lay their eggs in them, but most of the eggs die. In addition, the requirements of the larvae are not fully understood, so effective management of the rivers is difficult.

Common name Hellbender (mud devil, ground puppy, Allegheny alligator, big water lizard, devil dog)

Scientific name *Cryptobranchus alleganiensis*

Family Cryptobranchidae

Order Caudata (Urodela)

Size 12 in (30 cm) to 29 in (74 cm)

Key features Head and body strongly flattened; there is a wrinkled fold of skin along each flank; eyes small and gray; body yellowish brown or olive-green in color with irregular black spots, some of which may clump together to make larger blotches; eyelids absent

Habits Usually nocturnal; hides by day under rocks and submerged logs but also active in the day during rain, especially in the breeding season

Breeding Fertilization is external; females lay 150–400 eggs in an underground nest

Diet Mainly crayfish; small fish, other hellbenders, tadpoles, toads, and water snakes also recorded

Habitat Clear, fast-flowing mountain streams with no silt

Distribution North America from southern New York State to northern Alabama

Status Formerly common but becoming increasingly rare due to habitat destruction, silting, and pollution of the streams in which it lives

Similar species None in the region; the related giant salamanders of Japan and China (*Andrias japonicus* and *A. davidianus*) are similar but even larger

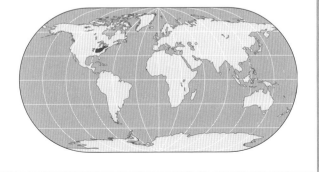

Hellbender *Cryptobranchus alleganiensis*

Hellbenders are bizarre and interesting inhabitants of the crystal-clear mountain streams flowing from the Appalachian Mountains of eastern North America. Their future is in doubt due to human activities.

LIKE THEIR CLOSE RELATIVES the giant salamanders, hellbenders require clear, shallow, well-oxygenated streams and rivers with a rocky bottom. They use the spaces between the rocks to hide in. Adults and juveniles require spaces of a different size, so a good mix of large rocks and smaller gravel is important. Flowing water keeps smaller particles from filling the gaps and also helps maintain a good level of oxygen in the water. If the river is dammed, if silt accumulates through disturbance on the banks upstream, or if the water is polluted by agricultural runoff, chemicals, or mining activity, the hellbenders disappear.

Night Feeding

Hellbenders spend much of the daytime hiding under rocks on the riverbed. They are territorial and rarely share a rock: Animals trying to crawl beneath an occupied rock are chased away. At night they venture out and crawl slowly over the bottom in search of food. Their main prey is crayfish, and they will eat up to four in one night; but they take a variety of other food as well, including small fish and fishing bait. They also eat each other, especially as eggs or larvae.

They appear to use a combination of sight and smell for finding food and will work their way upstream following its scent. They feed by means of a sideways snap or by simply opening their mouth wide, causing water (and prey) to rush into it. In captivity they will eat pieces of meat—the general feeling is that hellbenders will eat almost anything. They rarely wander far during a night's hunting and usually return to their own rock by morning. Average movement is about 30 to 60 feet (9–18 m), but males have larger home ranges than females.

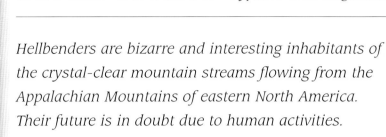

In suitable conditions hellbenders occur at high densities, with an estimated 10 animals per 120 square yards (100 sq. m) of stream in parts of the White River in Missouri. Estimates over the same area in other rivers range from one to six animals. Hellbenders occasionally leave the water voluntarily and may crawl up onto emergent rocks, but they never go far.

The color and pattern of hellbenders provide good camouflage against the jumbled rocks of the riverbed. The coloration is particularly effective against a scattering of dead oak leaves from overhanging trees in the fall, when they are more likely to be on the move during the day. Occasional animals are orange or reddish in color—the result of random mutations. They do not, as earlier writers believed, belong to a separate species that they called *Cryptobranchus fuscus*.

Hellbenders produce large amounts of slimy secretions from glands in their skin. The secretions deter some predators and parasites. They are bitter to taste and create a burning sensation if they come into contact with an open wound. Some predators seem to avoid hellbenders for this reason, but hellbenders of all ages are eaten by large fish, turtles, and water snakes.

⊕ *The ideal habitat for hellbenders is among rocks of varying sizes on the beds of shallow streams and rivers. They hide under the rocks by day and make nests beneath them in the breeding season.*

Breathable Skin

Hellbenders have lungs, but they hardly ever come to the surface to breathe because they can obtain nearly all their oxygen through cutaneous (skin) respiration. In experiments hellbenders were prevented from surfacing with no apparent ill effects, and one survived even after having its lungs surgically removed.

Most of their oxygen requirement is absorbed through the skin—the many folds and crenellations on the skin increase the surface area over which breathing can take place. The folds have a dense network of capillaries close to the surface and are, in effect, inside-out lungs. In quiet or warm water that is not well endowed with oxygen, hellbenders

sway from side to side, causing the skin folds to undulate. The movement probably serves to send the "jacket" of oxygen-depleted water away from the surface of the folds and replace it with more highly oxygenated water.

Young larval hellbenders have feathery external gills, which they lose at about 18 months old. The generic name *Cryptobranchus*, meaning "hidden gills," is therefore inaccurate—the young have gills that are not hidden, whereas the adults have no gills. Being smaller and lacking the numerous folds in their skin, the young probably need the external gills to extract enough oxygen from the water.

Breeding

Hellbenders have a complicated and unusual breeding system. Unlike in most salamanders (but as in frogs), fertilization is external. Males and females occur in roughly equal numbers. They are similar to each other, but males may have larger skin folds along

Adaptations

Despite their ungainly appearance and ponderous lifestyle, hellbenders are superbly adapted to the shallow, fast-flowing rocky streams in which they live. Their flattened shape offers little resistance to the flowing water, allowing them to work their way upstream and also to crawl into narrow spaces under rocks. Although their eyesight is relatively poor, they have light-sensitive cells over their whole body. Those on their tail are especially finely tuned and may help them position themselves safely under rocks without their tail poking out to give the game away. They have a good sense of smell and will move upstream in search of food such as a dead fish, following the trail of scent molecules. Smell is possibly their most important sense when hunting. They also have a lateral line similar to that of fish, with which they can detect vibrations in the water.

their flanks and on the outside of the legs, and females become swollen with eggs at the start of the breeding season. They mate in the fall, from late August through mid-November, with some variation depending on where they live.

At this time they become restless. They move around on the riverbed even during the day and may congregate in unusually large numbers. They poke around among the boulders, and males choose a brooding site to develop. It is a depression in the gravel, scooped out under a large, flat rock, with its entrance facing downstream. Once it is built, the males sit in the nest with their heads poking out, waiting for females. When a ripe female comes along, the male may emerge from the chamber to drive her in; and once there, he prevents her from leaving until she has laid her eggs. While she lays them in two long strings, the male positions himself to one side and sprays them with milt (fluid containing sperm). He waves his body from side to side and raises and lowers his hind legs as he does so in order to distribute the sperm thoroughly over the eggs. Females may take two to three days to lay their full complement of 150 to 400

⊕ *Hellbenders have an unjustified reputation among fishermen for driving some fish away and inflicting poisonous bites. In reality they are harmless and eat mainly crayfish, snails, and worms.*

eggs, by which time the two strings become entangled and appear as a single, twisted mass. Females and males often eat some of the eggs as they are laid. Once the female has finished laying, the male drives her away from the nest but remains there himself, presumably to guard them. He may also attract more females, and a single nest can contain 1,000 or more eggs, the record being 1,946.

The eggs hatch after 45 to 84 days, and the hatchlings have a yolk sac that nourishes them for a few months. They also have external gills that disappear after 18 to 24 months. They live in spaces in the gravel, moving up to small stones and rocks in shallow water as they grow. They take five to eight years to reach sexual maturity, with males maturing at a slightly smaller size than females. By the time they are adult, hellbenders have relatively few predators, and they can live for 25 to 30 years in the wild. The record for a captive is 55 years.

The largest hellbender captured was just over 29 inches (74 cm) in length, and the average length of adults is 12 to 15 inches (30–38 cm). There is a good deal of variation in size from one population to another. For instance, those from Arkansas are often more than three times as large as those from some Missouri populations.

Subspecies

Hellbenders are divided into two subspecies. The typical form, *C. a. alleganiensis*, is found over most of the species' range, but the Ozark hellbender, *C. a. bishopi*, is restricted to a small part of southeastern Missouri. The latter subspecies has a blotched rather than a spotted pattern and a darker chin as well as other, less obvious differences.

The origins of the name hellbender are unclear, but it seems that the animal has always aroused strong feelings. The specific name *alleganiensis* refers to the Allegheny Mountains where it lives. Apart from hellbender, other local names include mud devil, ground puppy, Allegheny alligator, big water lizard, and devil dog—none of them particularly complimentary.

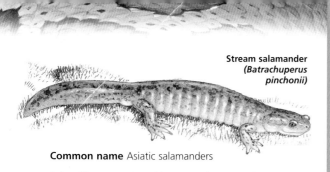

Stream salamander
(Batrachuperus pinchonii)

Common name Asiatic salamanders

Scientific names *Hynobius, Batrachuperus, Liua, Onychodactylus, Pachyhynobius, Ranodon,* and *Salamandrella* sp.

Family Hynobiidae

Order Caudata (Urodela)

Size 3 in (8 cm) to 7 in (16 cm)

Key features Small- to medium-sized salamanders; bodies slender; tails about the same length as the head and body combined; skin smooth and slimy with a series of about 12 grooves along the flanks (costal grooves); color mostly gray or brown, sometimes with mottled lighter and darker markings

Habits 8 species are aquatic; the rest are terrestrial and nocturnal for most of the year but aquatic in the breeding season, mostly in small ponds

Breeding In ponds or streams; a pair of egg sacs each containing 80–100 eggs attached to stones or plants; eggs fertilized by the male after the female has laid them; eggs hatch after about 40 days; larvae metamorphose after about 100–120 days

Diet Small invertebrates

Habitat Woods and meadows near streams and pools; aquatic species may live in streams or ponds

Distribution Asia

Status Some species are very rare

Similar species All other salamanders in the region have a granular skin and lack costal grooves

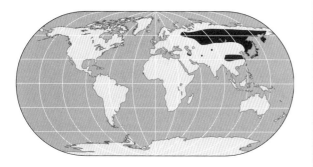

Asiatic Salamanders

Hynobiidae

The family Hynobiidae is the only family of salamanders that is exclusively Asian. Many are poorly known, and a few are extremely rare.

THE HYNOBIIDS ARE CONSIDERED to be primitive salamanders because they practice external fertilization. The only other family that does this is the giant salamanders, Cryptobranchidae. Hynobiids are easily distinguished from other salamanders in the region (the giant salamanders and the Salamandridae) by their smooth, slimy skin and costal (rib) grooves. They have well-developed lungs (apart from the two *Onychodactylus* species from Japan, which lack lungs altogether).

All hynobiid salamanders are secretive, living in wooded or grassy places, often near the streams or ponds in which they breed. Outside the breeding season they hide under logs, stones, or among leaf litter, but a few species stay permanently in the water.

Restricted Ranges

The stream salamanders, *Batrachuperus*, are found in small mountain brooks or springs in caves and are either totally aquatic or live within a few inches of the edge of the water. They all have very limited ranges in Iran, China, and neighboring countries—*B. gorganensis* is known from a handful of specimens taken from a cave on the shores of the Caspian Sea in Iran.

Another species, the Anji salamander, *Hynobius amjiensis*, occurs only in a damp meadow on top of Mount Longwang in China, surrounded by clumps of bamboo and pine trees. It breeds in nine small ponds each less than 1 square yard (1 sq. m) in area and about 18 inches (46 cm) deep. Estimates of the population put the number of breeding females at about 261. By contrast, the Siberian salamander, *Salamandrella keyserlingi*, is the most widespread salamander in the world, and

SEE ALSO Salamander, Japanese Giant **41**:30; Hellbender **41**:32

⊖ *A cave salamander,*
Batrachuperus persicus *from
Iran. Its body is typical of the
family, being smooth and slimy with
costal grooves on its side.*

Family Summary

Family Hynobiidae 36 species of Asiatic salamanders in 7
  genera:
Genus *Hynobius*—22 species from Turkistan and Russia to
  Japan
Genus *Batrachuperus*—7 species from western China, Tibet,
  Afghanistan, and Iran
Genus *Liua*—1 species from China, the Wushan salamander,
  L. shihi
Genus *Onychodactylus*—2 species, the long-tailed clawed
  salamander, *O. fischeri* from northeastern Asia, and the
  Japanese clawed salamander, *O. japonicus*
Genus *Pachyhynobius*—1 species, the Shangcheng stout
  salamander, *Pachyhynobius shangchengensis* from China
Genus *Ranodon*—2 species from Central Asia, including the
  Semirechensk salamander, *Ranodon sibiricus*
Genus *Salamandrella*—1 species, the Siberian salamander,
  S. keyserlingi

H. chinensis, the Chinese salamander,
also has a wide range over central
and eastern China. Its estimated
population on Zhoushan Island,
which has an area of about 190
square miles (500 sq. km), is
about 4,000 individuals.

Larval Phase

All species go through an aquatic
larval phase before metamorphosing
into adults. The breeding of the
Chinese salamander has been well studied
and is probably typical of *Hynobius* species.
Breeding continues throughout the winter from
mid-November until early March.

Females lay a pair of egg sacs that are
curved and slightly spiral in shape, each
containing about 80 to 100 eggs. The male
then straddles the egg masses and fertilizes
them by releasing sperm. They take about 40
days to hatch, and the larvae metamorphose in
100 to 120 days.

Life in the Freezer

The Siberian salamander lives from the Ural
Mountains to Kamchatka and across Siberia and
Mongolia to Manchuria and North Korea. The
species is notable for being the most widely
distributed salamander in the world, with a
range of over 12 million square miles (31
million sq. km). In the northern part of its range
it is only active for three to four months of the
year, when it migrates to its breeding ponds on
the tundra and steppe.

The Siberian salamander has a remarkable
ability to tolerate freezing conditions, and the
adults can survive temperatures as low as -40°F
(-40°C). They do this by producing "antifreeze"
chemicals in their blood and tissues. On several
occasions salamanders found frozen in the
permafrost have been "revived" by thawing.
The salamander can also be active when it is
only a fraction of a degree above freezing, and
even its spawn can survive being frozen in ice
for short periods.

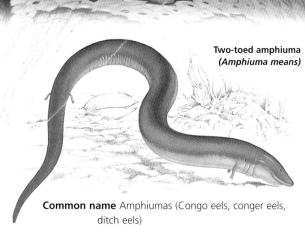

Two-toed amphiuma
(*Amphiuma means*)

Common name Amphiumas (Congo eels, conger eels, ditch eels)

Scientific name *Amphiuma* sp.

Family Amphiumidae

Order Caudata (Urodela)

Number of species 3

Size Up to 39 in (100 cm)

Key features Very elongated and eel-like; body cylindrical; legs tiny and vestigial with 1, 2, or 3 toes according to species; eyes small with no eyelids; external gills lacking, but pair of gill slits present just behind the head; color gray, paler underneath, with no markings

Habits Completely aquatic

Breeding Females lay long strings of 50–150 eggs and remain with them until they hatch

Diet Almost any aquatic organisms, including crayfish, frogs, fish, water snakes, and snails

Habitat Ponds, ditches, swamps, and slow-moving streams

Distribution Southeastern North America (the coastal plain from eastern Texas to southeastern Virginia)

Status Common (*A. means* and *A. tridactylum*); *A. pholeter* is rare

Similar species The 3 species resemble each other greatly, but otherwise they could only be confused with eels (however, eels have fins, because they are fish)

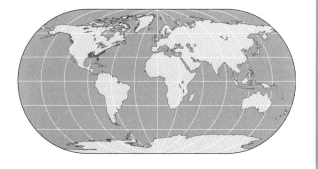

Amphiumas

Amphiuma sp.

Anyone who can count to three can distinguish between the three different species in the family, which is made up of the one-toed, two-toed, and three-toed amphiumas.

AMPHIUMAS' LIMBS ARE little more than tiny, spindly appendages that are slightly ridiculous and probably redundant. The legs have regressed through natural selection as the animals' lifestyle has evolved. Like the eels they resemble, amphiumas are aquatic. They live in burrows and forage through heavily vegetated or mucky water. Limbs would get in the way; and since they have become reduced, there is little need for toes either.

Despite this, they do occasionally leave the water and travel across land, and have been seen crossing roads. During droughts they burrow into the mud to estivate, and adults can survive for up to three years without feeding. Amphiumas have lungs and lack external gills but retain the gill slits (the openings through which gills emerged at the larval stage).

Amphiumas are thought to have occurred over a much wider range in North America as recently as the upper Miocene period (up to 5.3 million years ago) but retreated to the southeastern coastal plain in the Pleistocene period, 1.8 million to 10,000 years ago (the period during which humans evolved and spread). They are found nowhere else in the world, probably as a result of their specialized requirements for still or slow-moving water systems choked with vegetation or decaying matter. They often take over crayfish burrows, perhaps after having eaten the occupant, or rest among the roots of water hyacinths.

Egg Laying and Development

The two-toed amphiuma, *A. means*, is the most common and widespread species. It lives in Florida and neighboring states as far north as southeastern Virginia. The three-toed species,

⤴ *Amphiuma means*, the two-toed amphiuma, is the largest of the amphiumas. Its tiny legs are completely out of proportion to its body size and are easy to overlook, leading people to confuse these salamanders with eels.

SEE ALSO Frogs and Toads **42**:8; Snake, Southern Water **49**:80

A. *tridactylum*, is similar and apparently very closely related (but, of course, it has three toes). Females of these species and presumably also of the rare one-toed species, A. *pholeter*, lay 50 to 150 eggs in burrows or cavities that they first make for themselves.

The females lay their eggs in the winter and then coil around them until they hatch, which takes place several months later in summer. In the meantime, the water level may have fallen, so that by the time the eggs hatch, the nest cavities are above the water level along the edges of the pools or ditches in which they live. This may not be typical, however, because nest cavities that are not exposed are almost impossible to find.

The larval stage does not last long, and the larvae lose their external gills after about three weeks. They become sexually mature at about four to five years old and have been known to survive in captivity for up to 27 years.

Looking to the Future

Populations of the two- and three-toed amphiumas are probably quite healthy despite the loss of most of the wetlands in the southeastern United States owing to development. Habitat destruction affects some regions more than others. The one-toed amphiuma, however, has a much more limited range in southwestern Georgia and adjacent parts of northeastern Florida. Within this region populations are localized, and there is no opportunity for the salamanders to move from one to another. They are rare (or, at least, rarely seen), and there is some concern over their future.

Feeding and Defense

Amphiumas of all species are not fussy eaters. They prey most heavily on whatever animal is most common where they live. Often that is crayfish, but they also eat earthworms, fish, insects and their larvae, snails, and even clams, snakes, and turtles. Their main method of defense is to give a painful bite, but they also have a layer of slime covering their bodies that makes them difficult to grasp.

California giant salamander
(*Dicamptodon
ensatus*)

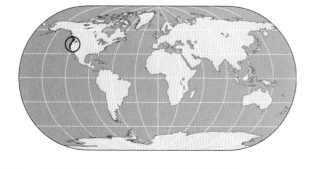

Common name Pacific giant salamanders

Scientific name *Dicamptodon* sp.

Family　　Dicamptodontidae

Order　　Caudata (Urodela)

Number of species 4 (Cope's giant salamender, *D. copei*;
coastal giant salamander, *D. tenebrosus*;
California giant salamander, *D. ensatus*; Idaho
giant salamander, *D. aterrimus*)

Size　　7 in (18 cm) to 13 in (33 cm)

Key features Adults large and stout with broad, slightly
flattened heads and raised eyes; gray or
brown in color, with a dark, mottled pattern;
some never metamorphose and remain as
large larvae throughout their lives—they have
bushy external gills, 4 legs, and low tail fins
that start level with the hind limbs

Habits　　Nocturnal; metamorphosed adults are
terrestrial, larvae are aquatic

Breeding　Where known, females lay clusters of eggs in
underwater cavities

Diet　　Aquatic and terrestrial invertebrates; larger
prey, such as small mammals and lizards; also
cannibalistic

Habitat　　Larvae live in woodland streams; adults live
alongside the streams in old-growth forest

Distribution North America in coastal central California
and the Pacific Northwest

Status　　Becoming rarer as their habitat is destroyed
by clear-cutting and subsequent silting up of
forest streams

Similar species Tiger salamanders are similar but do not
occur alongside the Pacific salamanders

　SEE ALSO Salamander, Tiger **41**:64

Pacific Giant Salamanders

Dicamptodon sp.

*Pacific giant salamanders are only found in the Pacific
Northwest of the United States and in a small part of
neighboring British Columbia, Canada. They are very
secretive, often burrowing down into thick moss or
underground chambers. Their larvae live in streams
and are more easily found than the adults.*

OF THE FOUR SPECIES of Pacific giant salamander,
three are almost identical. In fact, they were
formerly regarded as a single species,
Dicamptodon ensatus. The fourth species,
Cope's giant salamander, *D. copei*, is distinct.
This salamander rarely transforms into an
adult and can reproduce while it is still a
larva, a process known as neoteny.
(Surprisingly, neoteny is quite
common in salamanders,
occurring occasionally in
the other three species

of *Dicamptodon* as well as in members of several other families.) Cope's giant salamander is, therefore, a tadpole for the whole of its life and has fins along the top and bottom of its tail and external gills, although they are very small.

The other three species, once they have metamorphosed into adults, are large and chunky. Their heads are very wide but flattened, with small eyes positioned on top. Their roughly cylindrical bodies have a row of folds down either side, known as the costal grooves, and their limbs are powerful because they use them for digging.

Adults are found under logs, bark, and rocks but never far from streams or the edges of mountain lakes. They also climb and sometimes reach heights of over 7 feet (2 m) in shrubs and trees.

Specialized Habitats

All the Pacific giant salamanders (including Cope's giant salamander) occur in very specialized habitats in the states of California, Oregon, Washington, Idaho, and British Columbia. Due to the westerly winds that bring moist air from the Pacific Ocean, these regions have a high rainfall. Over the ages the conditions have created forests of tall conifers dripping with mosses and lichens, drained by thousands of small, clear, cold streams that run down to the coast. At higher altitudes in the Rocky Mountains there are numerous small mountain lakes that also contain cold, well-oxygenated water. The forest floor is littered with rotting stumps and fallen trunks. The decaying wood is home to insects and other invertebrates, as well as small mammals.

The adult salamanders live on the forest floor during the nonbreeding season. They hide in burrows, especially during dry spells in the summer months, and emerge onto the surface only on wet, cool nights, mainly in the winter and early spring. In the spring they migrate from the surrounding forest to congregate around springs at the sources of streams, where they lay their eggs in chambers under the ground.

The larvae live in small- to medium-sized forest streams and mountain lakes. They are well

⊕ *A coastal giant salamander,* **Dicamptodon tenebrosus, crawls on the forest floor in the Cascade Mountains of Oregon.**

adapted to life there and spend most of their time on the bottom of the streams, among gravel and other sunken debris. They seem to prefer the downstream sides of pools and backwaters that occur along the watercourses. They absorb much of their oxygen and get rid of up to 80 percent of their waste carbon dioxide through their skin, which accounts for their small gills.

Where conditions are suitable, they can occur in large numbers, and in places they are the most numerous vertebrate species. The larvae take two or more years to metamorphose, and so the streams in which they live must be permanent. The forests help maintain the streams because they absorb rainwater like a sponge and release it slowly throughout the year.

Opportunistic Feeders

Adult Pacific giant salamanders are voracious feeders. Although their main prey are probably slugs, worms, and other invertebrates, they regularly take small mice and shrews. Amphibians are also eaten, including other salamanders and even smaller members of the same species. Although it is hard to study such secretive amphibians, Pacific giant salamanders almost certainly feed at night, when they emerge during rain showers to forage over the surface. However, while they are in their underground retreats, they probably feed opportunistically by capturing worms or other small animals that happen to enter the chambers in which they shelter.

The larvae are also aggressive feeders. Bearing in mind how large they can grow—to 12 inches (30 cm) in many cases—they are able to tackle just about any aquatic invertebrate. In addition, they eat fish and the eggs and tadpoles of other amphibians that share their habitat. They include the rare tailed frog, *Ascaphus truei*, whose tadpoles form

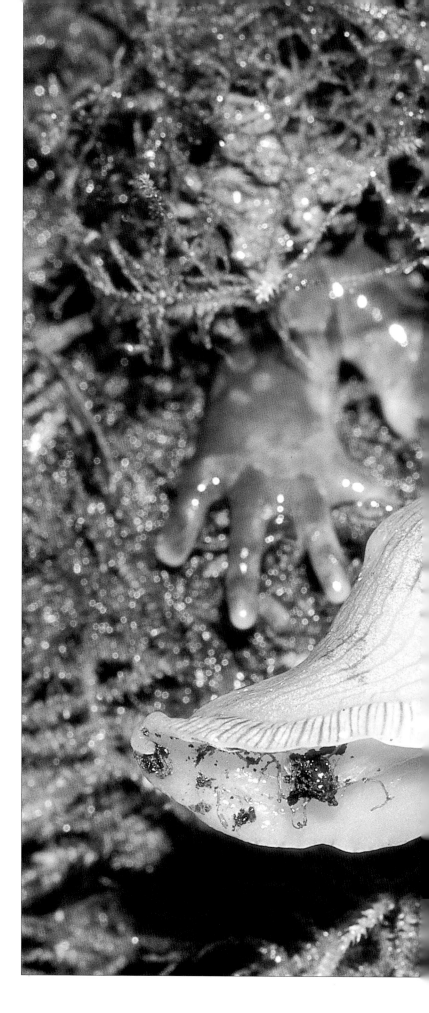

⊖ *A California giant salamander, Dicamptodon ensatus, eats a large banana slug. Invertebrates, small mammals, and lizards are also included in their diet as adults.*

14 percent of the diet of some populations of *D. ensatus*; the tadpoles of the northwestern salamander, *Ambystoma gracile*, make up 39 percent of their food. *Dicamptodon* larvae eat just about anything they can get their mouths around (although in experiments they spat out the larvae of rough-skinned newts, *Taricha granulosa*, which produce poisonous substances in glands in their skin). Pacific giant salamander larvae can even be caught on a hook and line— once they grab prey in their jaws, they will not let go and can be lifted out of the water.

Because they are not very discriminating and feed in response to movement, adult and larval Pacific giant salamanders often eat one another. When they are attacked on land, whether by a member of their own species or a different predator, they arch their back and hold their body high off the ground by stretching their legs out and standing on the tips of their toes. If this doesn't frighten off the predator, they lash out with their tails, which are covered with poisonous secretions. At the same time, they make loud rattling or growling sounds. They can also give a painful bite, using sharp, curved teeth. Larvae have little defense against predation, however, and the females stay with their eggs and newly hatched larvae for several months to defend them.

Reproduction

Courtship has not been observed in Pacific giant salamanders, but the adult males and females move toward the headwaters of streams and springs in the breeding season (which can be in spring or fall depending on the species). They probably find each other by following scent trails.

Mating is thought to be similar to the mole salamanders, Ambystomatidae, to which they are closely related. Fertilization is internal, and during courtship the male encourages the female to pick up a small parcel of sperm, the spermatophore, in her cloaca.

Before laying her eggs, the female digs down into the gravel at the bottom of a stream until she finds a suitable chamber or cavity

A Conservation Issue

As with many threatened animals, habitat loss is the greatest threat to the Pacific giant salamanders. The forests of redwood, Douglas fir, and hemlock where they live are known as "old-growth" forests, meaning they contain trees 250 years old or older, along with younger trees and fallen logs. The largest trees can reach 300 feet (91 m) high and over 6 feet (1.8 m) in diameter, and in places the canopy cover can be up to 80 percent, providing constant shade and cool conditions on the forest floor and in the forest streams.

Old trees, young trees, dead trees, and fallen logs all provide microhabitats for a wide range of animals whose lives are linked together. On the forest floor they provide all the microhabitats needed by the salamanders: high humidity, rotting logs and stumps to hide in, and cool, clear streams in which to breed.

Old-growth forests of this type only occur in the moist regions of the American Pacific Northwest and are the key to the continued survival of the salamanders. They were more extensive in former times, perhaps covering 15 to 17 million acres (6–7 million ha) across Oregon, Washington, and neighboring states. European settlers cleared large areas for farming and timber. More recently, commercial logging operations have reduced the area of forest even further, and now there are only about 2.4 million acres (1 million ha) left at most. Almost 90 percent of the old-growth forest has been destroyed. About half of what is left is protected in national parks or wilderness areas. The rest is earmarked for more logging. Scientists worry that when the logging is finished—in about 25 years—good habitat will be too fragmented, and the salamanders and other animals will not be able to move around freely.

Pacific giant salamanders only occur in old-growth forests or in similar habitats that are equally threatened. In particular, logging activities cause mud and silt to get into the streams. The mud clogs the gills of the salamander larvae and also makes it hard for them to find prey. After an area has been logged, the population of salamander larvae downstream falls dramatically a few years later.

The forests also provide the right habitat for a wide variety of other unique plants and animals, some of whose life cycles are linked with the salamanders in ways that we do not yet fully understand. They include the rare tailed frog, *Ascaphus truei*, several other rare salamanders, and most famously of all, the northern spotted owl, *Strix occidentalis caurina*.

It was concern over this owl in the 1970s that started an argument between the logging companies and conservationists that is ongoing. The logging companies would like to take all the large trees from the old-growth forest, and the conservationists would like to stop logging altogether. Until they can find a compromise, the future of this unique and interesting habitat and of the Pacific giant salamanders will be uncertain.

⊖ *A California redwood forest floor is an ideal hiding place for the California giant salamander,* Dicamptodon ensatus. *Unfortunately, such habitats are disappearing.*

between the rocks, using her powerful front limbs and tough, horny toes. Then she lays her eggs one at a time, attaching them individually to rocks or pieces of sunken wood. The eggs are large and white, and quite numerous.

One nest of *D. tenebrosus*, for example, contained 83 eggs, and another contained 146 eggs. Details of the eggs of the other three species are not known, but they are likely to be similar. The females stay in the water near the eggs until they hatch. This can take several weeks or even months, and the larvae also grow and develop very slowly. They may remain in the water for two or three years, growing to 12 inches (30 cm) in length before they finally change into adult salamanders and leave the water for a life on the land.

A small number of Pacific giant salamander larvae never metamorphose at all. Instead, they stay in the water throughout their entire lives. In the case of Cope's giant salamander the larvae rarely metamorphose—only four adults have ever been found, even though the larvae are quite common.

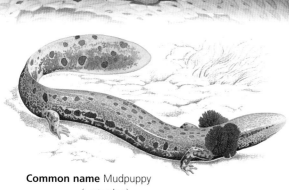

Common name Mudpuppy (waterdog)

Scientific name *Necturus maculosus*

Family Proteidae

Order Caudata (Urodela)

Size 8 in (20 cm) to 20 in (50 cm)

Key features Adults take the form of larvae with 3 pairs of branched, bushy external gills and with tail fins; wide, flat head with small eyes; body flattened from top to bottom; color brown with lighter speckled markings; larvae have a pair of yellow stripes down the back

Habits Totally aquatic; unable to survive long out of water

Breeding External fertilization; female lays her clutches of 60–120 eggs in underwater cavities in the spring or summer; eggs hatch after 38–63 days

Diet Aquatic insects and their larvae, crustaceans, amphibians, and fish

Habitat Rivers, lakes, ditches, and streams

Distribution Eastern North America from southeastern Canada into the eastern United States but not along the coastal plain

Status Common in suitable habitat

Similar species The hellbender lacks external gills as an adult and occupies a different type of habitat; could possibly be confused with other mudpuppies (waterdogs), but they are smaller, their ranges do not overlap, and they are all comparatively rare

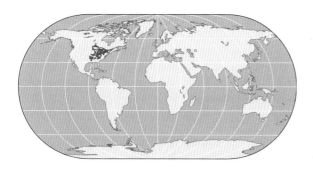

Mudpuppy

Necturus maculosus

Mudpuppies are the bulldogs of the amphibian world, tolerating a wide range of conditions and eating anything they can fit into their mouths.

THE USUAL HABITAT OF MUDPUPPIES includes canals and ditches choked with vegetation or mud, as well as flowing rivers with gravel bottoms and lakes with clear, cool water. In muddy waters they may be active during the day as well as at night, groping their way through the muck in search of food. In clearer waters they hide in the day under logs and rocks or in burrows, and only emerge at night. They have been found 60 feet (18 m) below the surface of lakes and may be active under ice if the lakes or ditches freeze

Waterdogs

There are five species of mudpuppies, or waterdogs, all living in North America. Although *Necturus maculosus* is very common and wide ranging, the other four (all known as waterdogs) have more limited ranges. The Alabama waterdog, *N. alabamensis*, lives in Alabama and adjacent states. The Gulf Coast waterdog, *N. beyeri*, occurs as two separate populations: one along the border between Texas and eastern Louisiana, and the other from central Louisiana to Mississippi. The Neuse River waterdog, *N. lewisi*, has a small distribution in North Carolina; and finally, the dwarf water dog, *N. punctatus*, occurs from southern Virginia to Georgia.

All four of these species are smaller than the common mudpuppy, *N. maculosus*, but can be difficult to tell apart from each other. Whereas the common species occurs inland, the others all live on the coastal plain, along river systems draining into the Atlantic seaboard or the Gulf Coast. Little is known about their natural history, but they are thought to be similar to the mudpuppy in many respects. They seem to prefer (or require) rivers and streams with log-jams and pockets of accumulated leaf debris on the bottom in which to hide. They tend to be less active in the summer, perhaps because there is less food for them, or it could be to avoid predation from fish. Populations of some species are getting fewer and smaller, possibly due to pollution of their river systems.

over. Ohio fishermen fishing through holes in the ice often catch mudpuppies on baited hooks. In Lake Michigan and possibly elsewhere they migrate from the edges of the lake in spring and move back into deep water again during the summer.

Breeding

Mating occurs mostly in the fall but carries on throughout the winter, the timing varying according to location. After mating, the females retain the sperm in their tracts until the following spring or early summer and lay their eggs in May or June. They make nest sites in shallow water by scraping out shallow depressions under rocks, logs, or sunken trash, with the entrance holes facing downstream.

They attach the eggs singly to the underside of the roof of the cavity, turning upside down to do so. An average clutch consists of 60 to 120 eggs, and the female stays to defend them against predators until they hatch around 38 to 63 days later. The larvae prefer water that is still or moving slowly and often hide in submerged leaf litter, feeding on small invertebrates. They reach breeding size in about five years, by which time they measure around 8 inches (20 cm) in length.

Mudpuppies are successful salamanders that can occur at high densities in suitable habitats. Not so long ago they were collected in large numbers for dissection in university laboratories—a single catch in Michigan in the 1920s contained over 2,000 mudpuppies. Some authorities think that they might be important predators on fish eggs, possibly affecting commercial catches, but studies to investigate these claims have not been conducted.

⊕ **Necturus maculosus *is the largest of the mudpuppies (or waterdogs). It is aptly named—*Necturus *comes from the Greek word for swimming,* nektos, *while* maculosus *is the Latin word for speckled or mottled.***

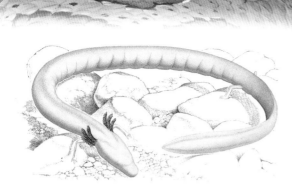

Common name Olm (white salamander, human fish)

Scientific name *Proteus anguinus*

Family Proteidae

Order Caudata (Urodela)

Size 8 in (20 cm) to 12 in (30 cm)

Key features Body elongated with spindly legs and a short tail; head has a blunt, rounded snout; eyes are covered with skin; even adults have bright-red, feathery external gills; body lacks pigment unless it has been exposed to light, in which case it is brown or black; 1 subspecies that lives near the surface is permanently black

Habits Totally aquatic

Breeding Fertilization is internal; females lay up to 70 eggs attached to the underside of a rock

Diet Aquatic invertebrates, especially freshwater shrimp and insect larvae

Habitat Underground streams and lakes in karst limestone formations

Distribution Southern Europe from extreme northeastern Italy through southern Slovenia along the Croatian coast and western Bosnia; also introduced populations in the French Pyrenees

Status Seriously threatened by pollution in many locations

Similar species None

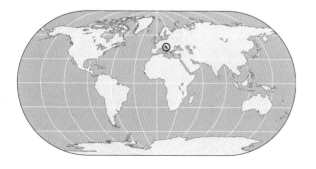

Olm

Proteus anguinus

The olm is one of the world's strangest animals. It lives its entire life deep in the bowels of the earth in the underground waterways that riddle the limestone mountains of the Adriatic region.

CAVE SYSTEMS PROVIDE some of the most stable environments in terms of temperature and water chemistry but have obvious drawbacks for animals trying to make a living in them. Most obviously there is no light, making it impossible to see anything. Most cave-dwelling creatures, whether they are newts, fish, or invertebrates, have reduced or nonexistent eyes. They use other sense organs to hunt their food and find their way around. The corollary is also true: Since they cannot see anything, nothing can see them, so most cave dwellers have no pigment and are white or pink in color.

Although the olm may look like an albino, it is not (but it lacks pigment); if individuals are taken out of their cave systems and exposed to light, they will gradually develop pigment until, after two or three months, they become black. If the animal is taken back down into the cave, the pigment will gradually disappear. The subspecies *P. a. parkelj*, which lives near cave entrances, is naturally pigmented and has visible eyes, but how functional they are is unknown.

Lifestyle and Breeding

Living in cold water that never exceeds 48°F (9°C) even in summer, olms have a low metabolism and very slow growth. They take seven to 14 years to reach maturity and live to great ages. They rarely need to feed and can survive long periods of fasting, the record going to one that lived for 12 years without eating.

Visitors to the caves around Postojna in Slovenia can see olms, but only the marginal populations living on the floors of the large caverns—most of the animals live in narrow subterranean channels that are inaccessible to humans. Natural history observations on wild

⊕ *The unusual-looking adult olm,* Proteus anguinus, *has red feathery gills and tiny legs. Its body appears to lack pigment, and it seems to have no eyes on its head. The eyes are, in fact, covered with skin.*

SEE ALSO Mudpuppy **41**:46; Newts and European Salamanders **41**:88

olms are practically impossible, but a colony of captive olms in a subterranean laboratory in the French Pyrenees gives us a good idea of their lifestyle. Adults congregate in wide cracks or under submerged rocks, but in the breeding season males become aggressive and territorial. They chase off other males and display to visiting females by fanning their tails, presumably to waft chemical hormones (pheromones) toward them. Eventually the male deposits a spermatophore, which the female takes into her cloaca to fertilize her eggs.

She attaches the eggs to the underside of a flat rock and remains nearby throughout the several months it takes for them to hatch. The newly hatched larvae have prominent eyes that later degenerate. Some reports mention females giving birth to live young—although that has not been confirmed, it may occur. Olms never metamorphose but are able to reproduce in the larval form. In other words, they are neotenous, like the only other members of their family, the mudpuppy, *Necturus maculosus*, and the waterdogs.

The olm occurs, or once occurred, in huge numbers in suitable habitats. There are old

The Human Fish

Not surprisingly, the sudden and unpredictable appearance of the strange olms was often viewed with some suspicion by local people. Back in the 17th century these amphibians were thought to be young dragons. The olm's pale colors, coupled with its small limbs, later led to an alternative name of the "human fish." It was formally described in 1768 by a Viennese doctor and zoologist, J. N. Laurenti, who named it *Proteus* for the Greek sea god who had the power to assume many forms.

records of them being used as fertilizer or pig food after having been swept out of their cave systems following heavy rain. The extent of their distribution under the porous limestone hills in which they live may never be known, but many populations are declining alarmingly. The main factors are industrial and agricultural pollution caused by chemicals percolating down through the limestone and accumulating in the water systems. Olms are internationally protected under CITES and have also been protected locally in Slovenia (formerly part of Yugoslavia) since 1947, but such measures have had little effect on their dwindling numbers.

⊕ *Olm eggs on a rock close to caves in the former Yugoslavia. The developing larvae can be seen inside the eggs.*

Common name Cascade torrent salamander

Scientific name *Rhyacotriton cascadae*

Family   Rhyacotritonidae

Order   Caudata (Urodela)

Size   3 in (7.5 cm) to 4.5 in (11 cm)

Key features Slender salamander with a small head,
                raised eyes, and a short tail; body yellowish
                brown above and yellow below with a
                distinct line where the 2 colors meet; back
                and sides covered with small dark spots

Habits   Secretive and nocturnal, hiding by day under
                stones at the water's edge

Breeding   Fertilization is external; females probably lay
                their eggs singly; eggs are relatively large

Diet   Not known but probably small terrestrial and
                aquatic invertebrates

Habitat   Streams and edges of streams in old-growth
                forest

Distribution Pacific Northwest (Cascade Mountains in
                Washington and Oregon)

Status   Rare

Similar species 3 other species of *Rhyacotriton* are
                virtually identical, and identification is only
                possible through distribution

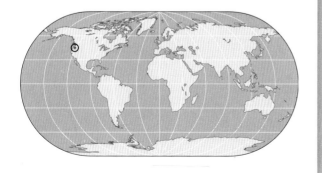

Cascade Torrent Salamander

*Rhyacotriton
cascadae*

*The Cascade torrent salamander and its three
close relatives are small, secretive salamanders
about whose lives little is known.*

CASCADE TORRENT SALAMANDERS live in the clear,
cold headwaters and springs of streams,
spending most of their time under partially
submerged moss-covered rocks or in fissures in
wet cliff faces. They probably come out at night
to forage for food but rarely wander far from
water. The farthest they are found from the
nearest stream is 50 yards (46 m). Their skin
contains toxic substances that are apparently
effective in driving off some predators, including
shrews. In defensive displays the salamanders
coil their tail, raising it off the ground and
waving it slowly backward and forward.

Small Clutches

Torrent salamanders have internal fertilization,
but courtship and the transfer of the
spermatophore from male to female have never
been observed. It seems that they breed
throughout the summer and fall, and breeding
tails off in the winter. This has been established
by examining females throughout the year to
see whether they contained eggs. During the
breeding season females contained from two to
13 eggs, with an average of eight. Although
the number of eggs is small compared with
many amphibians, each one is relatively large.

The eggs of *R. cascadae* have not been
found, but related species lay them singly and
place them in cracks in submerged rocks or in
cavities beneath them. Several females may lay
their eggs in the same place, since small groups
of eggs have been found together. The larvae,
which are slender and of the stream type (with
a flattened body and narrow fins), live in the
spaces between the gravel beds of the streams,
often in riffles, covered by less than 1 inch
(2.5 cm) of water. In favorable conditions larvae

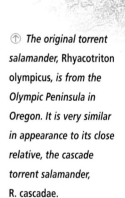

⊕ *The original torrent
salamander,* Rhyacotriton
olympicus, *is from the
Olympic Peninsula in
Oregon. It is very similar
in appearance to its close
relative, the cascade
torrent salamander,
R. cascadae.*

Cryptic Species

Until 1992 there was only one species of torrent salamander—the Olympic torrent salamander, *Rhyacotriton olympicus* from the Olympic Peninsula in Oregon. Close examination of this species revealed subtle differences, and three additional species were identified. They were not new in the sense that they had not been seen before, but their differences were so slight that they had been overlooked previously—one of them had been a subspecies.

When species are separated because of details that are difficult to see without looking at microscopic, biochemical, or genetic details, they are known as "cryptic," or hidden, species. The Cascade torrent salamander, *R. cascadae*, was one of the newly separated species. The other two were the Columbia torrent salamander, *R. kezeri*, and the southern torrent salamander, *R. variegatus*.

Coincidentally, around the same time—in 1989—scientists discovered that one of the other salamanders unique to the region, the Pacific giant salamander, *Dicamptodon ensatus*, was also in fact three separate cryptic species. The newly identified species were the Idaho giant salamander, *Dicamptodon aterrimus*, and the Pacific giant salamander, *Dicamptodon tenebrosus*.

occur at high densities—up to 40 per square yard (1 sq. m)—and rarely move more than a few feet. If they do move, they are more likely to work their way upstream than down. They feed on small aquatic invertebrates, and their growth rate is very slow: They are three to four years old before they metamorphose.

Torrent salamanders share their old-growth forest habitat with the Pacific giant salamanders in the family Dicamptodontidae, which probably prey on them. The felling of these forests is putting populations of both groups of salamanders at risk. Like the Pacific giant salamanders, the family of torrent salamanders is found nowhere else.

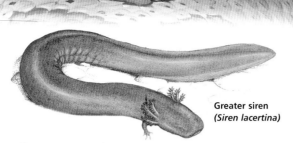

Greater siren
(Siren lacertina)

Common names Lesser
siren, greater siren

Scientific names *Siren intermedia, Siren lacertina*

Family Sirenidae

Order Caudata (Urodela)

Size Lesser siren: 7 in (18 cm) to 27 in (69 cm);
greater siren: 20 in (50 cm) to 35 in (90 cm)

Key features Both species eel-like except for a pair of
small front limbs with 4 small toes and
feathery external gills; gills are close to the
legs and sometimes obscure them; color dark
brown or olive with darker spots, sometimes
entirely black; larvae and juveniles of the
lesser siren often have a red patch on the
snout and another along the side of the head

Habits Totally aquatic; nocturnal

Breeding Fertilization probably external; female lesser
siren lays 200–550 eggs in a large clump;
greater siren lays up to 1,400 eggs singly or
in groups; eggs hatch after about 8 weeks

Diet Wide variety of prey taken, including
invertebrates, especially insect larvae, snails,
crayfish; they also eat some vegetation and
amphibian eggs, including their own

Habitat Swamps, marshes, ponds, and ditches—the
main requirement being plenty of mud

Distribution Lesser siren: southeastern North America
from the Mexican border on the Gulf Coast
to southeastern West Virginia and inland
along the Mississippi Valley; greater siren: a
more limited range within the same area

Status Common in suitable (but dwindling) habitats

Similar species The small front legs and absence of hind
legs distinguish them from all salamanders
except the dwarf sirens, which are much
smaller

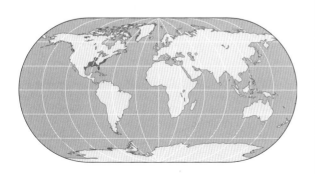

Sirens

Siren sp.

The mythical sea nymphs after which these salamanders were named sang to lure sailors to destruction on the rocks they inhabited. A vivid imagination is needed to see any similarities between the two!

THERE ARE TWO SPECIES of sirens in the genus *Siren,* and they are found in the southern and central United States and northeastern Mexico. Sirens are at home in the mud and are rarely seen. Unlike their mythical namesakes, they do not sing. Instead, they vocalize with a range of clicks and squeaks whenever they leave their burrows to come up for air. The sounds are thought to be a form of communication and may have a territorial function. When grasped, sirens often make a yelping sound.

Mucous Cocoons

Sirens live in almost any body of still water that is choked with vegetation or that has a good layer of decomposing leaves or mud on the bottom. The young live in shallower water than the adults. If the water dries up, neither the adults nor the young take to the land in search of somewhere else to live. Instead, they burrow down into the mud. If the mud dries out, the mucous coat covering their skin hardens to form a parchmentlike cocoon that covers the entire body except for the mouth and keeps the sirens from dehydrating. They remain inactive until the water returns.

Because they hoard large fat reserves in their tails, greater sirens, *S. lacertina,* can survive many months without feeding. The record is just over five years. Their metabolism slows down to 30 to 40 percent of its normal level while they are estivating, and they may lose three-quarters of their body weight. Lesser sirens, *S. intermedia,* also estivate but can only survive a few months in this state. Estivating

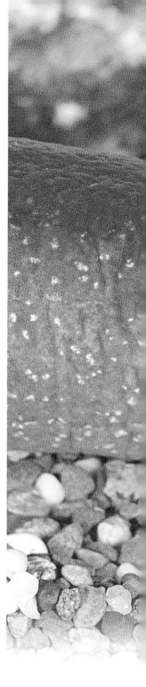

sirens are sometimes plowed up in fields that were previously flooded.

Despite the size difference, the two species have very similar lifestyles. During the day adults hide in underwater burrows built in mud banks or beneath sunken logs. At the end of each burrow is a chamber where the salamander coils when it is resting. Sirens are most active in the summer months when the water temperatures approach 86°F (30°C) and tend to forage just after dusk and immediately before dawn.

Instead of teeth, sirens have a horny beak, and they feed by suction, drawing water and prey into their mouth at the same time. Young animals live in dense clumps of vegetation through which they move at night in search of food. They eat mainly insect larvae and other invertebrates, including mollusks, but their stomachs often contain algae and pieces of plant material, perhaps ingested accidentally.

Egg Development

Courtship and mating have never been observed in either species, but evidence points to external fertilization, since in captivity eggs laid in isolation fail to develop. (If fertilization were internal, some eggs laid shortly after capture could be expected to be fertile. However, this is not the case, which indicates that fertilization occurs during, or after, laying.) Furthermore, eggs are rarely seen. Those that

⊕ The greater siren, Siren lacertina, is the largest of the sirens—the name lacertina means "little lizard." It has external gills, tiny front feet, and no back legs. Its tail has a fin above and below.

Dwarf Sirens

The family Sirenidae contains two other species of aquatic sirens, *Pseudobranchus axanthus* and *P. striatus*. They are 4 to 10 inches (10–25 cm) long and are known as dwarf sirens. They are similar in appearance to the larger sirens, but their front legs have only three toes each, and they have yellow or tan stripes running along their back and sides. They live in a wide range of water bodies from Florida to South Carolina, but they seem to be most common in small ponds and ditches that have a thick covering of water hyacinth, *Eichhornia crassipes*. In most respects this introduced weed is a menace. Dwarf sirens use their gills and skin to breathe in well-oxygenated water; but because water hyacinth reduces the oxygen-carrying capacity of the water, they also use their lungs for breathing, coming up to the surface periodically for air.

Like the other sirens, dwarf sirens sometimes live in ponds and swamps that dry up occasionally, in which case they burrow beneath the surface and estivate, reducing their metabolic rate by 50 percent or more to save energy. Estivating dwarf sirens shrink their gills, and their skin becomes dry. They can survive like this for at least two months. Living in ponds with low oxygen levels, and which may dry up occasionally, may actually benefit dwarf sirens because such conditions are unsuitable for predatory fish that would otherwise eat them. Other predators include wading birds, water snakes, and young alligators.

The breeding habits of dwarf sirens are unknown. They are assumed to have external fertilization because the males do not have the glands with which to form spermatophores, and females do not have an organ in which to store it (a spermatheca). Females lay their eggs in the winter and attach them to water hyacinth roots. In the absence of water hyacinths they use submerged aquatic plants. Nothing is known about their subsequent development.

Until recently there was only one species of dwarf siren, *Pseudobranchus striatus*, with several subspecies. However, one subspecies, *P. s. axanthus*, was promoted to a full species in 1993 based on differences in its chromosomes. These two species and the greater and lesser sirens, *Siren lacertina and S. intermedia*, make up the whole of the family Sirenidae.

The relationship of members of the family to other salamanders is a puzzle that herpetologists have yet to solve. The difficulty is that they have several primitive features, such as external fertilization, but anatomically they are similar to some of the more advanced salamanders. They also have some unique features, for example, a horny, beaklike structure instead of teeth.

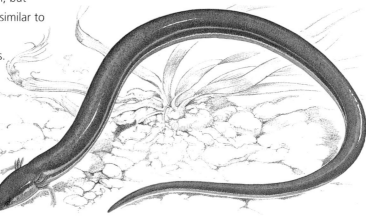

⊖ *The smallest of its family, the dwarf siren,* Pseudobranchus striatus, *lives among dense, submerged vegetation. It is nocturnal and feeds on tiny invertebrate animals that it finds among the plant debris near the bottom of the water.*

have been discovered have either been dredged up among aquatic plants or been found in depressions in mud on the bottom of ponds.

There have been too few observations to know if the two species have similar egg-laying habits. Both are prolific, however—the lesser siren laying up to 550 eggs, and the greater siren up to 1,400. They may be laid in large or small clumps or deposited singly. The egg-laying season appears to be late winter (in Florida), and the eggs hatch about two months later.

Lesser sirens probably mature after about two years. Their predators include water snakes, herons, egrets, large fish, and alligators, although the nocturnal habits of the sirens probably help keep predation to a minimum.

Habitat Loss

Although neither species of siren is rare, the loss of wetlands due to drainage is a problem. Also, measures to control flooding of low-lying land probably prevent sirens from dispersing across flooded areas to colonize new systems.

Mole Salamanders

The mole salamanders (family Ambystomatidae) are found only in North America from Alaska and Canada to Central Mexico. The family gets its common name from one species, *Ambystoma talpoideum*, the mole salamander from the southeastern states. *Talpoideum* derives from *Talpa*, the mole in the order Mammalia, and alludes to the burrowing habits of this species of salamander, which are shared by most of the others. Therefore "mole salamander" can refer to the species or the whole family.

All 30 species are contained in a single genus, *Ambystoma*, but some scientists think that four Mexican species may be different enough to be placed in a separate genus, *Rhyacosiredon*. The tiger salamander, *A. tigrinum*, has the largest range in the family, from Canada to Central Mexico almost from coast to coast. Other species, such as the California tiger salamander, *A. californiense* (sometimes regarded as a subspecies of the tiger salamander), the streamside salamander, *A. barbouri*, and some of the aquatic Mexican species, have very limited ranges. Mole salamanders have a thickset, chunky body and limbs. The head is wide and flattened with a rounded snout and raised eyes.

Terrestrial adults live in burrows or under leaf litter, logs, and other forest debris but return to ponds, marshes, and sluggish streams to breed in the fall, winter, or spring depending on species. They feed on a variety of invertebrates, and the larger species are able to tackle small vertebrates. They recognize their prey mainly by sight and stalk it in a slow and deliberate manner before catching it using their protrusible, sticky tongue. The tongue can be extended to up to 8 percent of their body length, and the whole process of opening the mouth, shooting out the tongue, and withdrawing it with prey attached takes just one-tenth of a second.

Having such a wide collective distribution, the mole salamanders have adapted to an equally wide range of conditions. The Jefferson salamander, *A. jeffersonianum*, and the spotted salamander, *A. maculatum*, for example, are tolerant of cold and can be active at temperatures only a fraction of a degree above freezing (32°F or 0°C). These species may get caught out in the breeding season if the weather suddenly turns cold in early spring, but they can survive under the ice if their ponds freeze over. At the other extreme Mabee's salamander, *A. mabeei* from the eastern coastal plain, tolerates higher temperatures than any other salamander—up to 100°F (38°C). Other species, such as the long-toed salamander, *A. macrodactylum*, may form aggregations during dry spells to reduce the effects of dehydration.

Forever Young

One characteristic of the mole salamander family (but not exclusive to it) is the occurrence of "axolotls." They are larvae that do not metamorphose. Instead, they continue to grow and eventually reproduce while still having larval characteristics. Strictly speaking, the term "axolotl" should be reserved for the Mexican mole salamander, *A. mexicanum*, which nearly always fails to metamorphose, but the name is often used to describe overgrown larvae of any of the species. This phenomenon is called neoteny, but some scientists distinguish between subtly different forms of neoteny, giving rise to a confusing array of terms. Certain species invariably retain larval characteristics and are known as obligate neotenics. They include the Mexican mole salamander and four other species from the same region. Other species produce only a proportion of neotenic larvae, sometimes

Common name Mole salamanders **Family** Ambystomatidae

Family Ambystomatidae—1 genus, 30 species of mole salamanders, including the Mexican mole salamander (or axolotl), *Ambystoma mexicanum*, and the tiger salamander, *A. tigrinum*; mole salamander, *A. talpoideum*

SEE ALSO Axolotl **41**:60; Salamander, Tiger **41**:64

⬆ *The Jefferson salamander,* A. jeffersonianum, *has long, slender toes and a slightly pointed snout. The species can hybridize with the blue-spotted salamander,* A. laterale, *sometimes making identification difficult.*

depending on environmental conditions. They are known as facultative neotenics and include the tiger salamander and the northwestern mole salamander, *A. gracile*.

Breeding

Most mole salamanders breed in the spring in response to thawing, increased water content in the soil, or rising

⬇ *The sight of a spotted salamander,* A. maculatum, *by a pond in Connecticut is a rare one, since the adults spend most of the time underground. These salamanders can live up to 20 years and may return to the same pond to breed each year.*

temperatures. But a few, such as the marbled salamander, *Ambystoma opacum*, and the ringed salamander, *A. cingulum*, breed in the fall. The marbled salamander is unusual in showing sexual dimorphism, the males being silvery white, while females are silvery gray. It lays its eggs in depressions in the ground that fill up with rainwater during the winter. They hatch and develop the following spring and summer. Most mole salamanders, however, congregate in ponds and ditches for courtship and

Females Only

Two mole salamanders are unisexual, all-female species. They arose when two species hybridized to form offspring with extra sets of chromosomes. The silvery salamander, *Ambystoma platineum*, contains two sets of chromosomes from the Jefferson salamander, *A. jeffersonianum*, and one set from the blue-spotted salamander, *A. laterale*. Similarly, Tremblay's salamander, *A. tremblayi*, contains one set from the Jefferson salamander and two from the blue-spotted salamander.

To start the development of their eggs, females of both kinds have to go through courtship and pick up the spermatophore of a male—a Jefferson salamander in the case of *A. platineum,* and a male blue-spotted salamander in the case of *A. tremblayi*—even though the sperm make no genetic contribution to the offspring. Strictly speaking, the scientific names of these "species" should be suppressed, because they are not true species. Scientists sometimes refer to them as JJL and JLL respectively, reflecting their parentage.

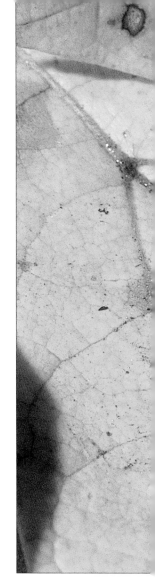

breeding. Males arrive at the pond first. Males of some species, such as the mole salamander, *A. talpoideum*, develop tail fins during the breeding season to improve their displays. Compared with the newts, however, they are not dramatic changes.

Aquatic courtship varies slightly among the species, but several common themes can be recognized. In four species there is a primitive form of amplexus, in which the male grasps the female. This may prevent other males from "stealing" their female—the male blue-spotted salamander, *A. laterale*, swims away from other males, taking the female with him. In other species there is no amplexus, and courtship takes the form of male displays. The display behavior is often stereotyped, although only a few species have been studied in detail.

The sequence of events in mole salamanders, *A. talpoideum*, for example, starts with a male approaching a female and nudging the side of her head before turning his attention to the base of her tail, which he also nudges. Mole salamanders have glands known as "hedonic glands" in that region, which are thought to release pheromones that stimulate or control courtship. The female contacts the male's cloacal region with her snout at the same time; and as both animals push against each other, they move in a circle. After one or two revolutions the male straightens up, and the female moves her snout to the tip of his tail, which he waves from side to side, brushing it against the female's head. He moves slowly forward, and the female follows. This

may continue for 10 minutes or more until the female moves forward to nudge the male's cloacal region once or twice. He stops waving his tail, deposits a spermatophore, and then moves forward again. The female crawls over the spermatophore and picks it up with her cloaca. If she is successful in picking up the spermatophore, the sequence is finished; if not, she follows him to try again.

Males may deposit several spermatophores in the course of a single courtship sequence, with up to 81 recorded for *A. maculatum*, the spotted salamander. On average the male spends only about one and a half minutes on each spermatophore, possibly to give other males less time to "muscle in" on the act.

Cheating Males

Even so, competing males often interfere with mating pairs by nudging the male or female, or both, to break the sequence and take it up themselves. Other males "cheat" by taking the female's place during the cloaca-nudging phase and depositing their own spermatophore on top of the one left by the first male, so that the female picks up the second one. This enables males to achieve matings without going to the trouble of courting females—they let another male stimulate the female but stand a good chance of their own sperm fertilizing the eggs. As well as speeding up the sequence, the first male may have another way to beat the cheats—by producing yet another spermatophore on top of the second one, so there are three spermatophores in the pile.

The female picks up several spermatophores during the course of a breeding season, since each one is only viable for a few hours (unlike in other salamander

Eggs and Algae

The egg clumps of the northwestern mole salamander, *Ambystoma gracile*, and probably other species as well, are often colonized by green algae, *Chlamydomonas* species, that live symbiotically with them, removing ammonia from the fluid surrounding them and producing oxygen. Compared with eggs without algae, the ones with algae develop more quickly and have a better survival rate.

↑ *The female marbled salamander,* Ambystoma opacum, *lays her eggs on land in places that normally fill with water during the fall. She stays with the eggs until the site floods, at which time the eggs hatch.*

families, in which spermatophores can be stored by females for up to 30 months). A spermatophore is good for only one batch of eggs. The female lays 12 or more batches over the course of several days. This presumably reduces the chances of losing them all to a predator or an accident. Mole salamander clutches, in total, are the largest among salamanders, with the axolotl, or Mexican mole salamander, *A. mexicanum,* laying up to 1,000 eggs, and some tiger salamanders laying 5,000 or more.

The female mole salamander makes her way to a submerged twig or the stem of an aquatic plant and grips it with her hind limbs, pressing her cloaca against it. Then she moves forward slowly and lays her eggs, which stick to the stem. The jelly layer surrounding the clutch begins to swell almost immediately, until the egg mass completely surrounds the twig or stem.

The resulting deep-bodied, pond-type larvae have high caudal and dorsal fins. They eat invertebrates, but they are also important predators of frog, toad, and other salamander larvae. Some tiger salamander larvae, and perhaps other species, are cannibalistic. Studies on several species show that young larvae sit and wait for their food on the bottom of ponds; but as they grow, their food requirements increase, and they need to search actively for it. That makes them more vulnerable to predation. Where several species live in one pond, they may avoid competition by foraging at different depths.

The larvae usually take two to five months to reach metamorphosis, but some species, especially certain populations of species such as the long-toed salamander, *A. macrodactylum,* that live in cold montane ponds, may overwinter and metamorphose the following spring.

Common name Axolotl (Mexican mole salamander, Mexican walking fish)

Scientific name *Ambystoma mexicanum*

Family Ambystomatidae

Order Caudata (Urodela)

Size 8 in (20 cm) but exceptionally to 12 in (30 cm)

Key features 4 limbs; 3 pairs of feathery external gills; high dorsal and caudal fins; head broad and flat; mouth has a wide gape; eyes small; wild-type axolotls are dark gray in color with scattered, small black spots; laboratory strains may be white or different colors produced by selective breeding

Habits Totally aquatic; more active at night

Breeding Females lay up to 1,000 eggs attached singly or in small clumps to twigs or aquatic plants; eggs hatch after about 2 weeks

Diet Aquatic invertebrates, including insect larvae and worms; fish and tadpoles

Habitat High-altitude lakes

Distribution Lake Xochimilco and Lake Chalco on the central Mexican plateau

Status Protected (CITES); Vulnerable IUCN

Similar species 4 other Mexican *Ambystoma* species (3 from central Mexico and 1 from Puebla) are axolotls and therefore similar in appearance

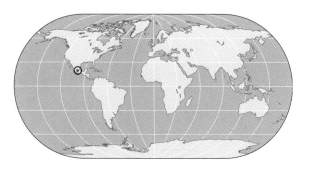

Axolotl   *Ambystoma mexicanum*

The axolotl is, in effect, an enormous tadpole. Adults retain many of their larval characteristics and can even reproduce as larvae.

THE AXOLOTL IS THE LARVAL FORM of the Mexican mole salamander, *Ambystoma mexicanum*. Its metamorphosis is incomplete: Although it develops small lungs and a reproductive system, it does not lose its external gills or the fins around its tail and along its back, and its skin does not take on characteristics of adult salamanders. Nor can it survive out of water.

Grown-up Axolotls

Metamorphosed axolotls are almost unheard of in the wild or in captivity. Although some sources maintain that an axolotl will metamorphose if the water level in its aquarium is lowered slowly, this is not so. Neoteny is a genetic trait in the axolotl, caused by low levels of iodine. Iodine is an essential component of hormones belonging to the thyroxin group, which are necessary for growth and development. Only by injecting axolotls with hormones of this type will they metamorphose (except in very rare cases, where they metamorphose spontaneously). Grown-up axolotls are very similar to adult tiger salamanders from Mexico, being dark gray with lighter mottling, and are closely related to them.

The axolotl's natural habitat is the montane lakes of central Mexico: Lake Xochimilco and Lake Chalco. Unfortunately, Lake Chalco exists no more, having been built over as Mexico City expanded southward. Lake Xochimilco survives as a network of canals and lagoons. It is under pressure from the growing human population nearby, but it is still rich in plants and animals.

Research Animals

The plight of wild populations of axolotls has led to the species being protected under CITES regulations and listed as Vulnerable by the

Aztec Connections

The axolotl's name has Aztec origins. It derives from two words: *atl,* meaning "water," and *xolotl,* meaning "monster." In Aztec mythology the god Xolotl was the twin brother of Quetzalcóatl, the plumed serpent god, but was disfigured and regarded as a monster. The local name for the species is *ajolote*, which has the same origins (bearing in mind that in Spanish the *x* and the *j* are pronounced as an *h).* *Ajolote* is also used for a completely different species, the amphisbaenian, *Bipes biporus* (a type of worm lizard), that lives in the Baja California region of Mexico. In pre-Hispanic Mexico the axolotl was a delicacy and was said to taste like an eel. Its fat was used as a medicine in the same way that cod liver oil is used nowadays.

IUCN. What is strange is that axolotls are bred in huge numbers by laboratories and amateur enthusiasts around the world. Axolotls were first bred in laboratories to provide material for teaching and research, especially in the field of embryology. They were suitable because they could be persuaded to lay fertile eggs at any time of the year and on demand. The jelly layer surrounding the eggs is also easy to remove, allowing cell division to be observed. Because of their wide availability scientists in other disciplines began to use them too.

Nearly everything we know about axolotls has been learned from captives. Wild populations, apart from being rare, are also difficult to observe. The first reference to them is in a book published in the early 17th century, but they were not named until 1789, as *Gyrinus mexicanus*. In 1830 the first reference to their local name and their eventual common name was made when they were renamed *Axolotus pisciformis*. In Paris in 1863 they were bred in captivity for the first time, and their strange life history was revealed.

⊖ *The white form of axolotl,* Ambystoma mexicanum, *is the most common. It is not a true albino because, although its skin lacks pigment, its eyes are black.*

Axolotls in Captivity

The most common axolotl is the white form, and there are probably more in captivity than in the wild. It is a genetic mutation in which pigment is lacking from cells in the skin but not from the eyes (known as leucisitic). There is an albino strain with pink eyes, but it has not been bred for as long as the white form and is seen less often. There are other, less distinctive varieties.

Axolotls need a spacious tank, but it does not have to be filled to the top—the most important factor is surface area. Axolotls eat earthworms, strips of lean meat, and other animal food. The young eat bloodworms, *Daphnia*, and pieces of each other; but the more often they are fed, the less they will mutilate each other. The tank bottom should be filled with large pebbles that the axolotls cannot ingest accidentally. They will use hiding places (broken crocks or drainpipes), but it is best to avoid building elaborate rock caves, because they are easily dislodged—sometimes with fatal results.

In the wild axolotls experience water temperatures of 41 to 68°F (5–20°C). Animals kept warmer than this will develop larger, more feathery gills but will also be prone to fungus and bacterial infections. A small filter helps keep the water clean, but axolotls dislike strong currents, so power filters should be avoided. The best way to keep them clean is to change about 20 percent of the water every week or so, using a siphon tube to take the water from the bottom of the tank. Rainwater is best; but if tapwater is used, it should be left to stand overnight before using it so that chlorine and other additives can disperse. If the replacement water is much colder than the water in the tank, the sudden temperature drop may stimulate breeding activity.

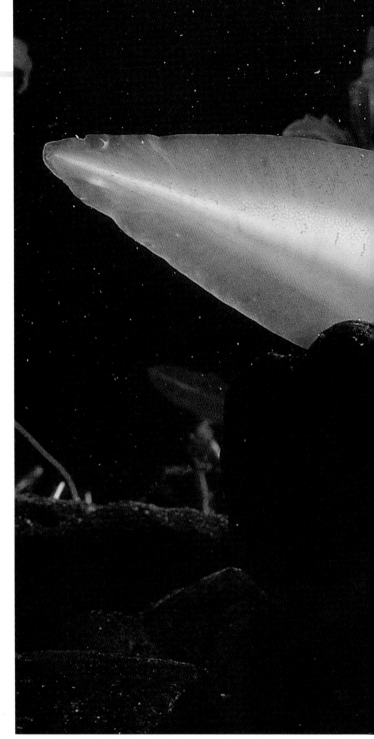

Breeding

Axolotls will breed at any time of the year, although a sudden drop in water temperature usually triggers courtship activity in males. Courtship includes nudging of the female by the male, after which she follows him until he deposits his spermatophore. Females start spawning a few hours later, laying their eggs singly or in small clusters, and attaching them to aquatic plants, twigs, or rocks. Larger females produce more eggs, and the clutch size can vary between 100 and 1,000 eggs. The eggs hatch after about two weeks, although the exact time varies with temperature. The young larvae are small at hatching and feed on very small aquatic creatures at first, such as young water fleas, *Daphnia*.

Axolotls have a characteristic method of feeding in which they remain motionless until a

suitable prey animal comes within range. Then they open their mouth so that water rushes in. At the same time, they move forward and upward slightly before sinking back to the bottom. As they grow, they become more voracious and often bite limbs and pieces of external gills from each other, especially during feeding frenzies. Under extreme circumstances a young axolotl can lose all four of its limbs. Far from being fatal, the loss does not seem to bother them, and the limbs eventually regrow.

Endangered Relatives

The axolotl is part of the tiger salamander group, but its closest relatives are the other four neotenic species that live in Mexican lakes. At least two of them are endangered—the Lake Pátzcuaro salamander, *A. dumerilii*, is listed in Appendix II of CITES, while the Lake Lerma salamander, *A. lermaense*, is listed by the IUCN as Critically Endangered. Shrinking habitats and pollution are the main reasons for the decline of these species.

⬆ *Axolotls are easy to keep in captivity, but their status in the wild is under threat. Today there are many more living in fish tanks than there are in Mexican lakes.*

Common name Tiger salamander

Scientific name *Ambystoma tigrinum*

Family Ambystomatidae

Order Caudata (Urodela)

Size 7 in (18 cm) to 14 in (35 cm)

Key features Head broad and flattened; mouth wide, eyes raised; limbs and feet short and stocky; tail relatively short and rounded in cross-section, although it becomes flattened from side to side in breeding males; males have slightly longer tails than females; coloration usually black, gray, or dark brown with lighter markings in yellow or cream or pale brown depending on the subspecies; neotenic individuals are common in some populations

Habits Terrestrial as an adult; nocturnal

Breeding Internal fertilization; females lay clumps of 5–100 eggs (the average is about 50) attached to aquatic plants or twigs; eggs hatch after 20–50 days

Diet Invertebrates and small vertebrates, including other salamanders; cannibalistic individuals occur

Habitat Forests, fields, meadows, and even desert and semidesert areas when breeding pools are available

Distribution North America, almost coast to coast, and from Canada to Central Mexico

Status Generally common, but some forms are extremely rare

Similar species Pacific giant salamanders, *Dicamptodon* species, the spotted salamander, *A. maculatum*, and other well-marked large species could be confused with tiger salamanders

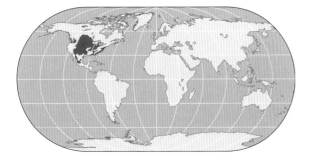

Tiger Salamander

Ambystoma tigrinum

The tiger salamander, which occurs in a wide variety of colors and patterns, is probably the most familiar salamander over much of the United States and Canada.

THE TIGER SALAMANDER IS divided into subspecies that vary somewhat in color and markings. Patterns include those in which black-and-yellow or black-and-cream areas are roughly equal in extent, with the lighter color arranged in irregular crossbars, for example, the barred tiger salamander, *A. t. mavortium*. In some subspecies the lighter areas are more extensive than the dark ones, as in the blotched tiger salamander, *A. t. melanostictum*, and in others the light markings consist of small round or oval spots distributed over the animal's body, for example, the eastern tiger salamander, *A. t. tigrinum*. Finally, there is a form in which the lighter markings are olive-green or gray, and the small black spots are hardly visible, as in the Arizona tiger salamander, *A. t. nebulosum*. Some of these local forms are widely distributed and are so common that they are used as fishing bait, whereas others are extremely rare and enjoy total state and federal protection.

Lifestyle Variations

As well as the color and geographical variations, there are variations in lifestyle within and between populations. Six forms, or "morphs," are recognized; some populations have only two, but others can include all six. For example, most tiger salamanders eat invertebrates and occasionally small vertebrates, but cannibalism is sometimes present in certain morphs. Cannibalistic salamanders can be immature larvae, mature aquatic larvae that fail to metamorphose (neotenous larvae), or terrestrial adults. The cannibalistic morph is usually larger than the normal morph and has a broader

⊕ *The barred tiger salamander,* Ambystoma tigrinum mavortium, *was named the Kansas State amphibian in 1994. As well as having bright yellow or olive spots, blotches, or bars on its back and sides, it has a distinctive "grin" on its face.*

head, larger skull, and an extra row of teeth. The teeth are longer than those of normal tiger salamanders and may be curved backward.

The different morphs are not evenly distributed across subspecies—cannibals are rare in the eastern tiger salamander, *A. t. tigrinum*, for instance. The barred subspecies, *A. t. mavortium*, varies in that some larvae metamorphose at a smaller size than others. The small larvae live in temporary pools and develop more quickly than the larger ones that live in permanent bodies of water. Like spadefoot toads, their development is probably accelerated so that they have a better chance of leaving their pools before they dry up.

In general, however, tiger salamander larvae grow slowly and can reach large sizes before metamorphosing, especially if they are not overcrowded and there is plenty of food to go around. Eastern populations are more likely to stay in the water for extended periods. They often reach sexual maturity shortly after they leave the water. They may travel

A Tiger Salamander Rarity

The rarest tiger salamander is *A. t. stebbinsi*. It lives on hillsides and meadows in the Huachuca and Patagonia mountain ranges in southeastern Arizona. The population was only recognized as a separate subspecies in 1988 when it was found to have been cut off from other tiger salamanders by large areas of unsuitable habitat. It breeds only in a limited number of cattle tanks and modified water holes. Historically it would have bred in naturally occurring water holes and springs, but about 90 percent of suitable habitat in the area has been lost, degraded, or altered. Several water holes where it was known to breed in the 1960s have dried up in times of drought, killing any larvae in them (although metamorphosed individuals living nearby may have recolonized them when they filled up again).

Disease killed all the salamanders at three sites in 1985, and diseased individuals were also found at another seven sites. An associated problem is the introduction of nonlocal species of amphibians, especially the American bullfrog, *Rana catesbeiana*, and fish, which may prey on the tiger salamanders or their larvae and can also spread disease. Larvae of tiger salamanders are widely used as fishing bait in Arizona, and subspecies from other parts of the state have been introduced to the area for bait propagation, so there is also a danger that the native form will be diluted by interbreeding.

several hundred yards after they leave the ponds, or they may remain nearby, perhaps returning to shallow water to feed on frog tadpoles and other aquatic prey. Adults sometimes migrate to temporary ponds even if they have already bred in permanent ponds, presumably because prey such as insect larvae and frog tadpoles become concentrated as the water evaporates. Such migrations, whether to breed or to move from one pond to another, nearly always take place during rainstorms in summer and fall.

In the west of their range tiger salamanders tend to live in the burrows of small mammals, but in the east they usually dig their own burrows with their powerful front limbs. The burrows are often only a few inches deep;

but an eastern tiger salamander was found 7 feet (2 m) deep, and a blotched tiger salamander in Alberta, Canada, was found using a rattlesnake den for shelter in the winter.

Life Cycle

The breeding pattern is typical of the family. Males may try to interfere with courting pairs by nudging the male or the female out of the way or by covering spermatophores with their own. Spermatophores are larger than in other mole salamanders. Males can lay up to 37 during a single night, but the average number is 21. Females lay their eggs singly or in clumps depending on subspecies, but an average egg mass numbers around 50 eggs, which are attached to twigs

⊕ *Adult Arizona tiger salamanders,* **Ambystoma tigrinum nebulosum,** *are brownish gray with small, dark spots. The subspecies is found in parts of Colorado, Utah, New Mexico, and central Arizona.*

A Close Relative

The California tiger salamander, *Ambystoma californiense*, used to be part of the tiger salamander complex, but most scientists now recognize it as a separate species. Its status is based on genetic studies, its geographic isolation from other forms of the tiger salamander, and its distinctive markings, which consist of round, lemon-yellow spots on a jet-black background. The species lives only in the Central Valley and a few localities farther west. Once widespread, now it is found only in small scattered colonies where suitable habitat still remains. Most populations have been eliminated due to urban and agricultural development. Another factor in its decline may be the programs to control ground squirrels and pocket gophers in the region: California tiger salamanders rely on the burrows of both species to retreat from the hot, dry California summers.

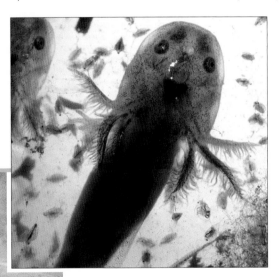

⊕ *California tiger salamander,* **Ambystoma californiense** *larvae, from the pools that occur during spring in a national wildlife refuge in California.*

and plant stems. In the north of the range total clutch sizes average 421 eggs, but farther south they are bigger—with 2,385 for small morphs and 5,670 for large morphs in Texas. The biggest recorded clutch was 7,651 eggs, the largest of any salamander.

The larvae are voracious feeders and can alter the ecology of their ponds by preying heavily on certain species of invertebrates. Even large larvae will eat small invertebrates, but they are capable of taking larger prey, such as frog tadpoles, when they are available. Cannibalistic larvae eat larger prey than typical larvae.

The growth rate of the larvae varies tremendously. In lowland ponds where the water is warm they usually transform in two to three months, after growing relatively quickly. Under extreme conditions the larvae in playa lakes in Texas can reach sexual maturity and transform when they are only five or six weeks old. In montane regions, on the other hand, they often overwinter and leave the water the following summer. Some fail to metamorphose at all, perhaps because the terrestrial habitat is more hostile than the aquatic one. Where they occur, cannibalistic larvae grow more quickly than normal ones and metamorphose sooner.

In summary, the life cycle of the tiger salamander is extremely variable. It changes with location (and therefore climate); but even at the same location some larvae are programed to feed more heavily, grow more quickly, and metamorphose sooner than others. However, larvae that take longer to grow usually metamorphose at a larger size. If the population contains cannibals, they are more likely to do well if the normal larvae vary in size (because they will be assured of suitable prey). In many populations some of the larvae do not metamorphose at all. They are neotenic—they become sexually mature while retaining some of their larval characteristics.

Lungless Salamanders

Common name Lungless salamanders **Family** Plethodontidae

Family Plethodontidae 2 subfamilies, 26 genera, and about 292 species

Subfamily Desmognathinae 2 genera:
Genus *Desmognathus*—16 species from North America, including the black-bellied salamander, *D. quadramaculatus*
Genus *Phaeognathus*—1 species, the Red Hills salamander, *P. hubrichti* from Alabama
(All these species have aquatic larvae as part of their life cycle, except the seepage salamander, *Desmognathus aeneus*)

Subfamily Plethodontinae 24 genera:
Genus *Aneides*—5 species from North America, including the green salamander, *A. aeneus*
Genus *Batrachoseps* —9 species of slender salamanders from western North America, including the California slender salamander, *B. attentuatus*
Genus *Bolitoglossa*—80 species from Central and South America
Genus *Bradytriton*—1 species, *B. silus* from Guatemala
Genus *Chiropterotriton*—12 species from Mexico
Genus *Dendrotriton*—6 species of bromeliad salamanders from Central America
Genus *Ensatina*—1 species, the ensatina, *E. eschscholtzii*, from western North America
Genus *Eurycea**—14 species from North America, including the three-lined salamander, *E. guttolineata*, the Barton Springs salamander, *E. sosorum*, and the dwarf salamander, *E. quadridigitata*
Genus *Gyrinophilus**—3 species of spring and cave salamanders from North America
Genus *Haideotriton**—1 species, the Georgia blind salamander, *H. wallacei* from underground springs in Georgia and northwestern Florida
Genus *Hemidactylium**—1 species, the four-toed salamander, *H. scutatum* from North America
Genus *Hydromantes*—3 species from North America
Genus *Lineatriton*—3 species from Mexico
Genus *Nototriton*—13 species from Central America
Genus *Nyctanolis*—1 species, *N. pernix* from Central America
Genus *Oedipina*—23 species from Central and South America, including *O. poelzi*
Genus *Parvimolge*—1 species, Townsend's dwarf salamander, *P. townsendi* from Mexico
Genus *Plethodon*—29 species from North America, including the northern slimy salamander, *P. glutinosus,* and Jordan's salamander, *P. jordani*
Genus *Pseudoeurycea*—35 species of false brook salamanders from Central America
Genus *Pseudotriton**—2 species of red and mud salamanders from North America, including the red salamander, *P. ruber*
Genus *Speleomantes*—7 species from Europe
Genus *Stereochilus**—1 species, the many-lined salamander, *S.marginatus* from southeastern North America
Genus *Thorius*—23 species from southern Mexico (many recently described)
Genus *Typhlotriton**—1 species, the grotto salamander, *T. spelaeus* from North America

(* species that have aquatic larvae as part of their life cycle)

The Plethodontidae is the largest family of salamanders by far. It contains about 292 species (some are still in dispute) out of a total of about 400 species of salamanders. It is divided into two subfamilies, the Desmognathinae and the Plethodontinae.

The Desmognathinae contains two genera and 17 species. *Phaeognathus* has just a single species, the Red Hills salamander, *P. hubrichti* from Alabama. The other genus, *Desmognathus*, has 16 species. They all occur in the United States and Canada, mostly in the Appalachian chain or the coastal plain to its immediate east and south.

All the other members of the family belong to the Plethodontinae, which contains about 275 species. They occur from southern Alaska and Nova Scotia in Canada through Central America into South America as far as eastern Brazil and central Bolivia. In addition, seven species of cave salamanders, *Speleomantes*, occur in southern Europe: three in northwestern Italy and parts of France, and four on the Mediterranean island of Sardinia.

Lungless Breathing

Although the family name Plethodontidae means "many teeth," the most distinctive characteristic of the family is their lack of lungs, hence the popular name of lungless salamanders. Because they have no lungs, they can live underwater without ever coming to the surface to breathe. Their loss of lungs may have evolved as a response to living in the cool, fast-flowing, highly oxygenated waters of mountain streams.

Many salamanders (and other amphibians as well) respire across their skin (a process known as cutaneous

The dwarf salamander, Eurycea quadridigitata, *lives on the edges of savanna ponds and swampy areas. It measures just under 4 inches (10 cm) long.*

Resting on liverwort leaves in cloud forest in Costa Rica, the worm salamander, Oedipina poelzi, *shows the smooth, glossy skin and elongated body that give it its common name.*

respiration) and through the lining of the mouth, which is well supplied with blood vessels. In most of these cases, however, cutaneous respiration is used as an additional system to supplement respiration using the lungs, and different species use the skin to varying degrees depending on their environment and other factors.

As a result of their total reliance on cutaneous respiration, lungless salamanders tend to be small. The reason is that smaller organisms have a greater surface area to mass ratio, which provides them with a relatively large area over which gaseous exchange can take place. In addition, their elongated shape increases their relative surface area even more, which is why so many plethodontids are long and slender.

Gaseous exchange can take place efficiently only across wet or moist surfaces, which limits plethodontid salamanders to certain types of habitats—they cannot survive under dry conditions, even if temporary. Whereas other salamanders can lose up to 40 percent of their body weight through dehydration and still recover, the figure is 25 percent or less for lungless salamanders. In this respect their small body size and elongated shape work against them—they may have a greater area over which to breathe, but they also have a larger area over which to lose water. This pushes them even farther toward the need for wet or moist habitats and also explains why lungless salamanders are only seen on the surface in numbers during rainy nights. Despite this apparent handicap, plethodontids are not only the most numerous family in terms of species, but they also occur in higher densities than other salamanders. Studies have shown that under favorable conditions there may be up to two dusky salamanders, *Desmognathus fuscus*, for every square yard of forest floor.

Damp Habitats

Lungless salamanders live in many types of habitat, the main requirement being enough moisture. There are burrowing, terrestrial, semiaquatic, and fully aquatic species, as well as some that climb into shrubs and trees. Burrowing species have relatively short limbs, while others (such as some *Bolitoglossa)* are at home in the canopy of tropical forests and have webbed feet or squared-off toes with which they can cling to smooth surfaces such as leaves. Some species can even walk upside down on the undersides of leaves. The bromeliad salamanders, *Dendrotriton*, live in the vases and leaf axils of bromeliad plants (such as pineapple and Spanish moss) that festoon large tropical trees.

69

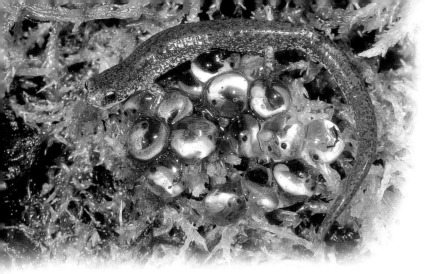

⊖ *Not a bug-eyed alien, but a closeup of* Ensatina eschscholtzii, *the ensatina salamander, in California. Its dark orange color blends in well with the leaves of the maple forests where it lives.*

⊖ *The female four-toed salamander,* Hemidactylium scutatum, *lays eggs attached to moss or other foliage near water in late winter or spring. She guards the nest until the eggs hatch six to eight weeks later.*

Some of the most important habitats for members of the family, especially those in North America, are seepages (sometimes referred to as flushes). They are areas (often the headwaters of streams and brooks) in which cool water emerges from underground springs and flows through rocks, soil, and moss. Seepages provide a constant supply of cool, highly oxygenated water throughout the year, and many small salamanders take advantage by living in and around these areas. They hide under rocks or among mud and vegetation, and lay their eggs there.

Salamanders of this kind can be thought of as semiaquatic, although many of them can survive away from water as long as the conditions are cool and moist. However, others live under the water for extended periods. Their eggs are often submerged but may also be placed in the splash zone, where humidity is close to 100 percent. As a rule of thumb, plethodontids with aquatic lifestyles have tails with a narrow keel, or ridge, along the top, giving them a triangular cross-section, but terrestrial kinds have tails that are round in cross-section.

Another favored habitat is caves, including artificial ones such as abandoned mine shafts. Many species that live in seepages and springs also extend their living space back into the caves from which the waters come. They include the well-named cave salamanders of Europe, of which there are seven species, previously placed in the genus *Hydromantes* but now referred to as *Speleomantes*. Others are more specialized and are always found in caves: They include several species in the genus *Eurycea*. They live in underground springs in Texas and Tennessee, and look very similar to the European olm, *Proteus anguinus*, a member of the Proteidae.

Chemical Communication

Plethodontid salamanders seem to live a life dominated by air- and waterborne odors. They have a shallow groove running from the upper lip to each nostril, called the nasolabial groove. It carries water containing chemical cues from wet surfaces to the nostrils, where it can be analyzed. The scents are used to establish territories, track females, and carry out other functions about which we can only guess. Associated with the nasolabial grooves, and probably supplementary to them, the males have a pair of small sensory swellings, or "cirri," on their upper lip. The males of some species only develop them during the breeding season, but they are permanent in others.

Males also have so-called courtship glands on various parts of their bodies, such as the chin (mental glands), and on top of the base of their tail. They are oval-shaped swellings that the male rubs over the female's body, especially her head and nostrils, during courtship. Males also have enlarged teeth that often become more developed during the breeding season. They use them to scrape or scratch the female's skin, allowing secretions from the glands to enter her bloodstream more easily.

Life Histories

Members of the Desmognathinae have aquatic larvae. The possible exception is the seepage salamander, *D. aeneus*, whose larvae sometimes hatch with gills that are lost a few days or weeks after hatching, and which do not feed. All the other species have larvae that live in a variety of aquatic environments and metamorphose after two months to a year. Within the other subfamily, the Plethodontinae, there are two types of life history. Members of the Hemidactyliini tribe go through an aquatic larval stage: The tribe contains the genera

Eurycea, Gyrinophilus, Haideotriton, Hemidactylium, Pseudotriton, Stereochilus, and *Typhlotriton*. Members of the other two plethodontine tribes (Plethodontini and Bolitoglossini) have no aquatic larvae, and their eggs hatch directly into small versions of the adults.

Elaborate courtship routines are characteristic of lungless salamanders, and in several species they include bouts of foot-paddling displays by males to females. Egg guarding by females is the norm. They regularly coil around their clutches, which are often laid on the undersides of rocks in or at the edge of water. In species that practice direct development, the incubation period can be quite lengthy.

⊖ *Courtship routines. The male* Eurycea bislineata *covers the female's skin with secretions and scrapes it with his teeth (1, 2); in* Plethodon jordani *the male leads the female and turns to slap his chin gland against her snout (3).*

Feeding

Lungless salamanders feed on a variety of small invertebrates, both terrestrial and aquatic, with which they share their habitats. Some terrestrial species have a method of feeding similar to that of chameleons. They have a long, protrusible tongue that can be shot out of their mouth using a complex arrangement of elongated cartilaginous structures in their mouth and throat. Their

range is impressive, and many species can reach food items that are nearly one body length away from them. The European cave salamanders, *Speleomantes*, are the most efficient, with a range of nearly 2 inches (5 cm).

Coloration

Plethodontid salamanders are typically brown or gray in color with occasional subtle markings in the form of speckles and with flecks of lighter or darker shades. A few species are more colorful, however. The green salamander, *Aneides aeneus*, is beautifully marked with yellowish green on a black background in an irregular, lichenlike pattern. *Ensatina eschscholtzii*, from the

American West Coast, has spots or bands of orange on a brown background. This species is divided into seven subspecies separated largely by their patterns.

Other species are red or have red backs, some of them warning predators that they secrete noxious fluids, while others act as mimics. Jordan's salamander, *Plethodon jordani*, is highly variable, with red-cheeked, red-legged, and silver-backed races found within a small area of the Appalachians. Experiments have shown that the red-legged and red-cheeked forms are distasteful to birds, but the silvery-backed form is less so, and the red color seems to act as a warning. Another species, the imitator salamander, *Desmognathus imitator*, also has a

⊖ *Jordan's salamander,* Plethodon jordani *(top), has bright red cheeks and is distasteful to birds. Its coloration is mimicked by the imitator salamander,* Desmognathus imitator, *whose cheeks are slightly paler red.*

species that have large ranges are declining, and their distribution is becoming patchy in places. Runoffs from coal strip mines pollute habitats downstream, and some systems that were home to many salamanders are now devoid of them. Other populations suffer from the draining of wetlands and acid-rain pollution. Species that are semiaquatic or that have aquatic larvae are more vulnerable than terrestrial species, although the latter also suffer from deforestation through removal of the leaf litter and reduction of the shade on which they rely. Research on the California slender salamander, *Batrachoseps attenuatus*, showed that the species was 10 times more abundant in old-growth forests than in regenerating forests, and there is similar evidence for several other species in the eastern part of the continent.

Other salamanders are relic species that have clung on in remote desert canyons and underground springs. They include the Inyo Mountain slender salamander, *Batrachoseps campi*, and the San Gabriel Mountain slender salamander, *B. gabrieli,* both from southern California and discovered only in 1979 and 1996 respectively. The latter species only occurs in two small areas of roughly 2.5 acres (1 ha) each.

All the *Hydromantes* and *Speleomantes* species have small ranges in areas with caves and underground streams, and many of the aquatic, pedomorphic *Eurycea* species such as the Barton Springs salamander, *E. sosorum*, survive as small, isolated populations. The Blanco blind salamander, *E. robusta*, was discovered in 1951 and has not been seen since, so it may be extinct.

Despite their seeming insignificance, small plethodontid salamanders often occur in large enough numbers to alter the ecology of areas by controlling small invertebrates and acting in turn as a food source for larger animals. Furthermore, they are so sensitive to pollution in many cases that they are useful "indicator" species, letting us know whether or not our environment is in a good state of health.

red-cheeked form, but only where it lives among the red-cheeked form of Jordan's salamander. Other species of plethodontids may also mimic this warning coloration in areas where Jordan's salamander is common.

Conservation

Plethodontid salamanders can be extremely common in suitable habitats, and some species are so numerous that they are collected for fishing bait. Elsewhere, however, lungless salamanders suffer from loss of habitat, especially through the clear-cutting of old-growth forests in the East and on the West Coast of North America. Pollution and the silting of forest streams also pose a threat. Even

Common name Black-bellied salamander

Scientific name *Desmognathus quadramaculatus*

Subfamily Desmognathinae

Family Plethodontidae

Order Caudata (Urodela)

Size 4 in (10 cm) to 8 in (20 cm)

Key features Stocky; appears rubbery rather than slimy; limbs well developed; 14 conspicuous costal grooves along its flanks; tail is flattened from side to side and has a ridge along the top; mainly brown in color, peppered with small spots of greenish yellow or rust brown, becoming overall darker with age; body black below

Habits Nocturnal; terrestrial or semiaquatic

Breeding Fertilization is internal; female lays small clutches of eggs on the undersides of rocks in shallow water; eggs hatch after 8–12 weeks into free-living, aquatic larvae

Diet Larvae eat small invertebrates, such as mayflies, stoneflies, beetles, ants, and bugs; adults eat a range of terrestrial prey, including other salamanders

Habitat Alongside, at the edge of, or in fast-flowing woodland streams

Distribution North America in the Allegheny Mountains from southern West Virginia to northern Georgia

Status Numerous in suitable habitats

Similar species Plethodontid salamanders can be difficult to tell apart, but the black-bellied salamander is one of the larger, more robust species of *Desmognathus*

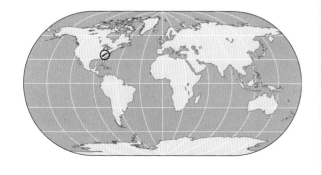

Black-Bellied Salamander

Desmognathus quadramaculatus

The black-bellied salamander and its close relatives live among waterfalls on the clear, boulder-strewn streams that drain the Appalachian mountain chain.

THE BLACK-BELLIED SALAMANDER is a robust, lively species and is one of the few plethodontids that may be active during the day. It is quick and agile; if disturbed, it darts away into a new crevice or into the water, where it may swim upstream. It lives along rushing watercourses, preferring small streams with plenty of large boulders, often in the vicinity of small cascades and waterfalls. Juveniles prefer slower-moving streams and seepages with plenty of stones of various sizes, which they use for cover.

Adults sometimes stray several yards from their streams, especially on damp nights, to hunt for food, but most individuals stay near the water in rock crevices or burrows in the bank. As they grow larger, they are less inclined to move and prefer to remain in or near their burrows, from where they ambush prey. They defend their burrows from other members of the species, and many have bite scars on their heads from fights. Over 40 percent of adults have lost their tails at some time.

Progressive Diet

The black-bellied salamander changes its diet markedly as it develops, thereby avoiding too much competition between the ages. Larvae eat small aquatic invertebrates, including the larvae of flies such as mayflies, stoneflies, and crane flies. Larger larvae also eat small crayfish and other salamander larvae. Juveniles usually stay in the water and eat flying insects when they touch the water's surface to breed, or when newly emerged. Adults eat a variety of terrestrial prey, including other salamanders, such as *Plethodon* and *Eurycea* species and the spring salamanders, *Gyrinophilus*. On the other

→ *Although nocturnal, the black-bellied salamander sometimes basks by day on wet rocks. It rarely ventures far from the side of a stream.*

SEE ALSO Salamander, Cascade Torrent **41**:50; Snake, Common Garter **49**:84

hand, black-bellied salamanders are preyed on by a wide variety of predators such as shrews and garter snakes, although they defend themselves by biting vigorously. Faced with a shrew, a black-bellied salamander opens its jaws to display the white lining of its mouth and lunges forward while snapping its jaws.

Eggs on Stalks

Courtship and mating have not been seen in this species but probably occur in late summer and fall. Females lay their eggs the next spring and attach them in layers or clumps to the undersides of rocks. Each egg is suspended by a short stalk, and two or more eggs may share a stalk. If the eggs are in contact with flowing water, they are constantly agitated and aerated by the current. The female stays with them until they hatch two or three months later.

The small larvae find shelter beneath and between stones on the streambed and grow slowly. They metamorphose after two to four years, by which time they will have reached about 1.6 inches (4 cm) from snout to vent, although at higher elevations they may develop more slowly and metamorphose at 2.1 inches (5.4 cm). They become sexually mature after a further five to seven years; so, including its larval stage, a breeding salamander may be 10 years old or more.

Interacting Species

The black-bellied salamander often lives alongside other species of *Desmognathus*, including the seal salamander, *D. monticola*, and the Ocoee salamander, *D. ocoee*. They probably prey on each other's young and also affect the population structure by competing for burrows and other cover. The seal salamander (and probably other species) uses chemical signals to detect other salamanders; if they are present, it may avoid them. Experiments in which one or more species of *Desmognathus* have been removed from a small area have yielded interesting results: Some species increase while others decrease, showing that they interact strongly, often in ways that are not yet fully understood.

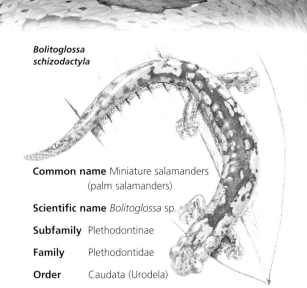

*Bolitoglossa
schizodactyla*

Common name Miniature salamanders
(palm salamanders)

Scientific name *Bolitoglossa* sp.

Subfamily Plethodontinae

Family Plethodontidae

Order Caudata (Urodela)

Number of species 80

Size 2.6 in (6.6 cm) to 10.2 in (26 cm) including
tail, depending on species

Key features Small- to medium-sized salamanders; body
slightly elongated; tail about the same length
as their combined head and body; limbs and
toes well developed; toes completely or
partially webbed; most are some shade of
brown, often with lighter brown, buff, or
yellow markings along their back

Habits Burrowing, terrestrial, or arboreal species

Breeding Fertilization is internal; eggs undergo direct
development and hatch after 4–5 months

Diet Small invertebrates

Habitat Humid forests

Distribution Central and South America

Status Some species are very common, others are
known from just a handful of specimens; they
are probably not rare, just difficult to find

Similar species Most other plethodontid salamanders
from the region are smaller and more slender

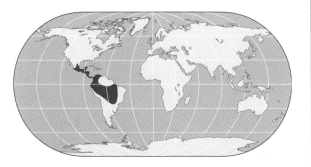

Miniature Salamanders

Bolitoglossa sp.

*Many humid forests in Central and South America
teem with miniature salamanders; but because they
are so secretive, they are rarely seen.*

WITH 80 SPECIES *Bolitoglossa* is the largest genus
of salamanders, and more are being discovered
almost every year. They must be among the
most difficult vertebrates to study because they
are extremely secretive, small, often well
camouflaged, and sometimes live in remote
regions. Many live in treetops where they are
practically inaccessible.

As a group they have taken full advantage
of a region in which there are few other
salamanders by exploiting a number of
ecological niches. Miniature salamanders may
live on the ground among forest litter, under
and inside rotting logs, or under mats of moss
and other vegetation on fallen or living
branches. They can also be found in shrubs,
among loose rocks on talus slopes, in epiphytic
plants, especially bromeliad plants that contain
a central vase ("tank bromeliads"), or in the
forest canopy. Canopy species are the most
difficult to study, and there must be many more
species at this level still awaiting discovery.
Hardly any have common names.

A researcher, J. L. Vial, made a thorough
study of *B. pesrubra* from Costa Rica, and much
of what we know about the genus comes from
his observations. He found them to be
semiarboreal at low altitudes but terrestrial at
higher elevations. They are most active at night,
and individuals from montane areas can tolerate
temperatures as low as 40°F (4°C) or lower in
some cases. They move very little from day to
day—over a six-month period he found that
juveniles moved on average only 9.1 feet
(2.8 m), adult females moved 12.1 feet (3.7 m),
and adult males moved 17.7 feet (5.4 m).

The species can occur at very high
densities, especially at high elevations, where

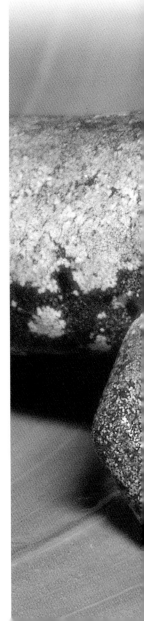

⊕ **Bolitoglossa
lignicolor** *in a rain forest
in Costa Rica. This tree-
dwelling species often
hides in bromeliad plants.*

Other Tiny Salamanders

There are a number of other plethodontid genera in Central America, the most important being *Nototriton* and *Oedipina*, with 13 and 23 species respectively. *Nototriton* differs most noticeably from *Bolitoglossa* in being smaller and in having pointed digits with only a limited amount of webbing. They live on the ground among moss or leaf litter, or in bromeliad plants. The smallest species is *N. richardi*, which only grows to a tiny 2 inches (5 cm) in total length, with its head and body being about half this. *Nototriton tapanti* is only a fraction bigger. Both species come from Costa Rica.

Oedipina species are extremely long and slender salamanders, reaching up to 10 inches (25 cm) in total, with the tail accounting for over 75 percent of the length. Their limbs are very small, and their minute digits are webbed. Most are burrowing, but some live under the bark of fallen trees, and some live in insect burrows in rotting logs. Others live in sand or gravel or under rocks near streams and rivers. As far as anyone knows, none of the *Nototriton* or *Oedipina* species care for their eggs.

Vial found there were over 9,000 salamanders per 2.5 acres (1 ha). Lower down there were fewer, 756 per 2.5 acres (1 ha), and densities were highest during rainy periods.

Size, Shape, and Color

The various species differ widely in size, with the smallest species (the appropriately named *B. diminuta*) growing to only 2.6 inches (6.6 cm), of which about half is its tail. It lives in the canopy among mats of moss and may lay its eggs there. The larger species, such as *B. robusta*, grow to 10.2 inches (26 cm), but most are around half that length. The females are larger than the males. In most species the tail is roughly the same length as the body and head combined.

Their feet and hands have varying amounts of webbing on them, which is closely correlated with habitat. Species that climb have fully webbed feet that act as small suckers on the smooth vegetation and allow them to grip rough surfaces. *B. epimila* can even walk upside down on the underside of leaves. Some climbing species

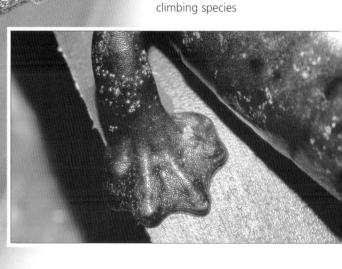

⊕ *Foot detail of the tropical palm salamander,* **Bolitoglossa dofleini,** *showing the webbing between the toes that helps the animal move over smooth vegetation.*

77

also have tiny claws at the tips of their digits, and most have prehensile tails to help them climb. Terrestrial or burrowing kinds have little webbing, however, and they often have rounded tips to their digits.

Most species are quite dull in color, helping them blend in with their surroundings. Perhaps surprisingly, there are no green species. Many have irregular brown, tan, buff, or light-gray markings along their backs. *B. striatula* is beige with irregular, narrow dark-brown stripes running along its back, giving good camouflage when it is resting among dead banana leaves by day or among other forest floor detritus. This species forages at night on shrubs, tall grasses, and reeds around the edges of ponds.

Bolitoglossa robusta is black or dark gray with a narrow light ring of cream, pink, or tan around the base of its tail, and *B. decora* is black, sometimes with a tan back and with large silvery-white blotches along its flanks. Other species are highly variable: *B. pesrubra*, for example, may be plain glossy brown, light gray to black, or it may be any of these colors with a pattern of lighter or darker spotting. The lighter areas may be pink or red, and the whole of its back may be brick-red, orange, or yellowish. Its limbs and throat may also be pink or red. It is hardly surprising that the species has been given several different names in the past.

Feeding and Defense

Miniature salamanders eat a variety of small invertebrates, which they catch with their protrusible tongue. Despite the apparent richness of their natural habitat, experiments with captives show that they grow up to five times faster than their wild counterparts, presumably because food is more readily available to them, and the effort involved in finding and catching it is less.

They are probably preyed on in turn by a number of birds, small mammals, reptiles,

⊖ **Bolitoglossa mexicana** *hangs upside down from a branch in a forest in Belize, using its prehensile tail to support itself.*

amphibians, and (probably) large invertebrates such as spiders and scorpions, although there is some evidence that noxious secretions from their skin deter some predators. In experiments garter snakes fed with miniature salamanders appeared to be distressed, and some were incapacitated. When faced with a predator, the salamanders may raise and display their tails, perhaps to warn of their secretions. *B. pesrubra* from low elevations raises its tail, whereas the same species from higher elevations (where there are no snakes) is less likely to do so.

All *Bolitoglossa* are able to shed their tails in an emergency, but some species are more likely to do so than others, judging from the numbers with regrown tails. In *B. pesrubra* only one salamander out of 81 shed its tail when a snake grasped it.

Breeding

The breeding season is extended, and the species that have been studied appear to breed continuously throughout the year. Male miniature salamanders are smaller than females and have long premaxillary teeth that protrude through their lips. They also have small swellings around their nostrils and a prominent gland, the mental gland, under their chin. During courtship males rub the gland on various parts of the female's body or introduce

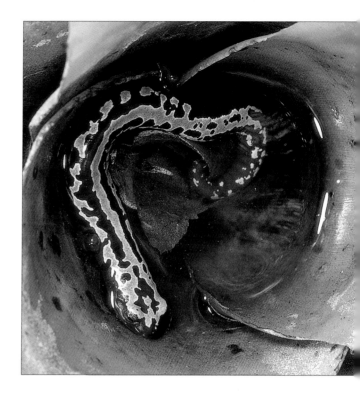

↑ **Bolitoglossa mexicana** *takes advantage of the rainwater that has collected in the vase of a bromeliad plant.*

its secretions into her body by biting her or breaking or scratching the skin.

Mating has not been observed in miniature salamanders. Clutch size probably depends on adult size, both across and within species. *B. pesrubra* lays 13 to 38 eggs, each about 0.2 inches (5 mm) in diameter, in cavities under rocks and logs and in the leaf axils of bromeliad plants. One of the parents—nearly always the female, but occasionally the male—coils tightly around the clutch with its head and chin resting on the eggs, and rotates them every few days using its tail and legs. The parent rarely leaves them—unattended eggs don't hatch.

The incubation period is 4 to 5 months, and as in all plethodontines, they undergo direct development. The young salamanders force their way out of the egg capsule when they are fully developed and measure about 0.8 inches (2 cm). They grow very slowly, and it can take 12 years for females and six years for males to reach sexual maturity. They may live for up to 19 years.

Tail Breaking

The mechanism of tail breaking is different in salamanders than in lizards and is known as pseudautotomy. The salamanders' tails do not have a fracture plane but have a constriction around the base, and breakage occurs there. (The bright ring around the base of the tail of *B. robusta* may mark the spot at which it breaks.) When a break occurs, the muscle and vertebral column break at a point closer to the salamander's vent than the skin does. This leaves a short cylinder of skin that closes over the wound to help healing and regeneration get under way.

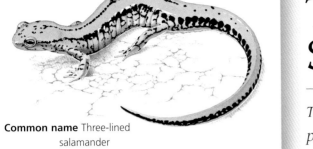

Common name Three-lined
salamander

Scientific name *Eurycea guttolineata*

Subfamily Plethodontinae

Family Plethodontidae

Order Caudata (Urodela)

Size 4 in (10 cm) to 7 in (18 cm) including tail

Key features Slender with long tail accounting for 60–65
percent of the total length; limbs well
developed; body has a pattern of three black
stripes, 1 on each flank and 1 down the
center of the back, on a tan or light-brown
background; central stripe stops at the base
of the tail, which is plain brown above

Habits Nocturnal; terrestrial

Breeding Fertilization is internal; female lays up to 100
eggs in winter; eggs hatch after 4–12 weeks

Diet Wide variety of invertebrates, including snails
and snail eggs

Habitat Forests; never far from streams, ditches, or
ponds

Distribution Southeastern North America along the
Appalachian chain onto the Coastal Plain and
up the eastern Mississippi Valley as far as
southwestern Kentucky

Status Common in suitable habitat

Similar species The species used to be a subspecies of
the long-tailed salamander, *E. longicauda*,
which is similar and whose range it abuts; the
two-lined salamander, *E. bislineata*, is also
similar but lacks the dark dorsal stripe

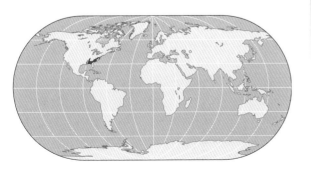

Three-Lined Salamander

Eurycea guttolineata

*The three-lined salamander is a typical terrestrial
plethodontid. It lives in forest litter or under logs
in hardwood forests, emerging on damp
and rainy nights to search for food.*

THE THREE-LINED SALAMANDER is most active during
the first few hours of darkness. Its diet is made
up of a long list of small invertebrates such as
beetles, flies, ants, spiders, crickets, and
caterpillars. Adults are not territorial and may
be found in groups.

The Reproductive Cycle

Their movements and breeding habits are
similar to those of the long-tailed salamander,
E. longicauda, with which they used to be
classified, but they may differ in small details.
Males are smaller than females, have elongated
teeth in their upper jaws, and tentacles (or
"cirri") below their nostrils. Adults feed
throughout the spring and summer, and in fall
they become less active on the surface.

Females move to breeding sites at that
time, seeking out springs, streams (or ponds
into which springs flow), caves, and abandoned
mine shafts. They lay their eggs in fall or in the
early spring, attaching them to the undersides
of rocks, either in flowing water or just above it.
Females have been found with small groups of
eggs, but it is not clear if they stay with them
until they hatch. They lay a total of 100 eggs.
Based on clutches that have been found, they
must lay them in several batches, which would
make egg guarding impossible. The eggs hatch
in four to 12 weeks depending on the water
temperature, so newly hatched larvae may
make an appearance in late fall or early spring.

The larvae live in cool springs, sometimes
in caves, and eat small invertebrates, especially
ostracods and copepods (minute aquatic
crustaceans such as *Daphnia* and *Cyclops*

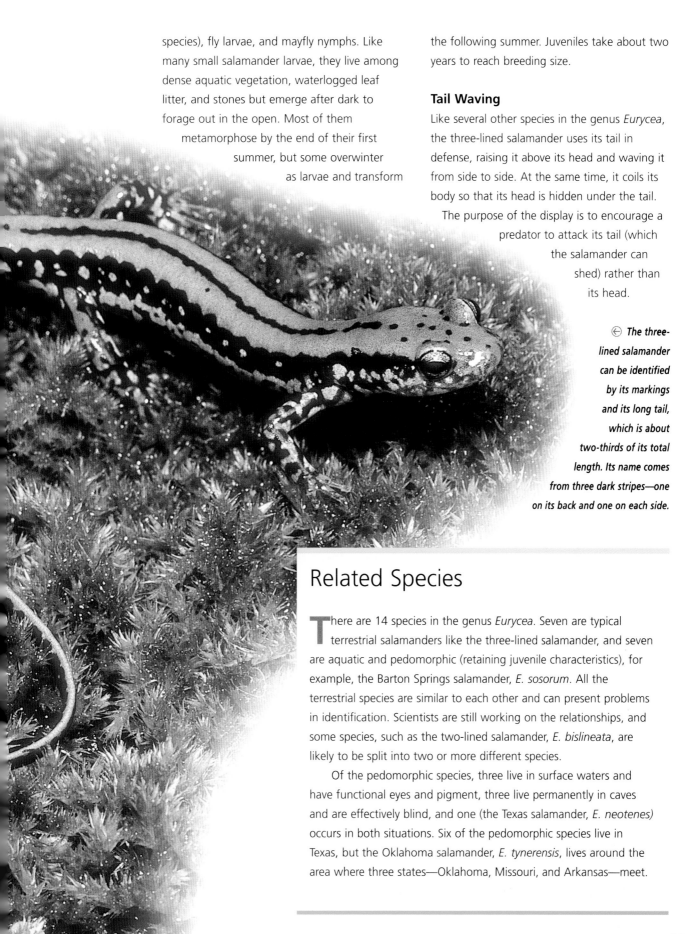

species), fly larvae, and mayfly nymphs. Like many small salamander larvae, they live among dense aquatic vegetation, waterlogged leaf litter, and stones but emerge after dark to forage out in the open. Most of them metamorphose by the end of their first summer, but some overwinter as larvae and transform the following summer. Juveniles take about two years to reach breeding size.

Tail Waving

Like several other species in the genus *Eurycea*, the three-lined salamander uses its tail in defense, raising it above its head and waving it from side to side. At the same time, it coils its body so that its head is hidden under the tail. The purpose of the display is to encourage a predator to attack its tail (which the salamander can shed) rather than its head.

⊖ *The three-lined salamander can be identified by its markings and its long tail, which is about two-thirds of its total length. Its name comes from three dark stripes—one on its back and one on each side.*

Related Species

There are 14 species in the genus *Eurycea*. Seven are typical terrestrial salamanders like the three-lined salamander, and seven are aquatic and pedomorphic (retaining juvenile characteristics), for example, the Barton Springs salamander, *E. sosorum*. All the terrestrial species are similar to each other and can present problems in identification. Scientists are still working on the relationships, and some species, such as the two-lined salamander, *E. bislineata*, are likely to be split into two or more different species.

Of the pedomorphic species, three live in surface waters and have functional eyes and pigment, three live permanently in caves and are effectively blind, and one (the Texas salamander, *E. neotenes)* occurs in both situations. Six of the pedomorphic species live in Texas, but the Oklahoma salamander, *E. tynerensis*, lives around the area where three states—Oklahoma, Missouri, and Arkansas—meet.

Common name Barton Springs salamander

Scientific name *Eurycea sosorum*

Subfamily Plethodontinae

Family Plethodontidae

Order Caudata (Urodela)

Size 2.5 in (6 cm)

Key features Gills external; legs spindly; snout distinctive and squared off; eyes small and pigmented; color variable, may be pale purple-brown, yellow, or cream with small flecks of color creating a mottled "salt and pepper" effect; groups of reflective scales appear as light patches

Habits Totally aquatic, living in deep water that stays at a constant 68°F (20°C)

Breeding Egg laying probably occurs in winter, otherwise habits not known

Diet Small aquatic invertebrates, especially amphipods

Habitat Springs in limestone rock formations, under rocks, in gravel, and among plants and algae

Distribution Four springs within Zilker Park, Austin, Texas

Status Extremely rare

Similar species Other pedomorphic salamanders occur in the area, including *E. nana, E. rathbuni, E. neotenes,* and *E. robusta*, but this is the only one that lives in Barton Springs

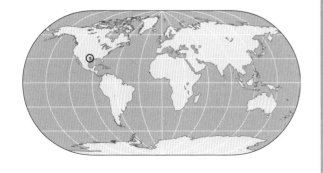

Barton Springs Salamander

Eurycea sosorum

The Barton Springs salamander was described to science only in 1993, but its existence was known as early as 1946. Today it is extremely rare and lives only in four springs within a small area of Austin, Texas.

THE BARTON SPRINGS SALAMANDER has a highly specialized lifestyle and a narrow ecological niche. In Barton Springs pool, for instance, it occurs only within a layer of gravel and small rocks overlying a coarse, sandy (or bare limestone) substrate near where the spring enters the pool. The water there is crystal clear, extremely pure, and contains no mud or silt.

Although nothing definite is known of the salamander's breeding habits, it is likely that they are similar to those of related species: Small numbers of eggs are probably attached to the stones and gravel on the bed of the stream or pool where it lives. Because of the low water temperature it takes a relatively long time for the eggs to hatch into tiny replicas of the adult.

The Barton Springs salamander is pedomorphic (meaning that the adults retain juvenile characteristics, such as external gills). There are other related pedomorphic species in the genus *Eurycea* from Texas and neighboring states, and some of them are restricted to underground streams.

Threatened Species

The Barton Springs salamander is extremely rare. Its known natural range is one of the smallest of any vertebrate species; and because it lies entirely within the city of Austin, Texas, there are grave concerns over its continued existence. A recent survey by the University of Texas using scuba equipment found only one individual. Furthermore, the salamander's continued survival depends entirely on the pristine water quality of the springs and the pools into which they empty.

ⓘ *Well adapted to its aquatic lifestyle, the adult Barton Springs salamander retains many juvenile characteristics, for example, its long, slender body, three pairs of external gills, and a relatively short, finned tail.*

Pedomorphic Relatives

The Barton Springs salamander is not the only rare pedomorphic species of *Eurycea* in Texas. The San Marcos salamander, *E. nana*, lives along the north bank of Spring Lake, which forms the headwaters of the San Marcos River in Texas. The Texas blind salamander, *E. rathbuni*, is a cave-dwelling species without functional eyes or pigment, also living near San Marcos. Both these species are endangered and protected by federal law, like the Barton Springs salamander. The Blanco blind salamander, *E. robusta*, is in the greatest danger, and it may already be too late to save it. Four specimens were found by a group of workmen opening up a spring in a dry riverbed in the Blanco River in 1951. The site was later filled in with gravel by the river, and the species has not been seen again.

The Texas salamander, *E. neotenes*, by contrast, is relatively common and well studied. It lives on the Edwards Plateau of central Texas (like the other pedomorphic forms) but has an extensive range throughout the system of caves and underground streams and the springs that emerge from the limestone.

The springs are fed by an underground lake, or aquifer, that extends to the south and west of Austin, and the rapid growth of the city is threatening to contaminate the watershed. The amounts of silt, heavy metals, petroleum by-products, pesticides, and other toxins entering the system have increased dramatically in recent years. The small invertebrates on which the salamander feeds (and therefore the salamander itself) are extremely sensitive to such changes. More specifically, a large multinational corporation wanted to develop a 4,000-acre (1,600-ha) site within the Barton Springs watershed despite overwhelming opposition from the citizens of Austin.

Amid accusations of corruption and intimidation, the Save Our Springs (SOS) movement was formed in order to fight any future development. The Barton Springs salamander become a symbol of the organization's efforts because it acts as an indicator for the water quality. The health of the salamander population is totally dependent on the health of the Springs, and so its scientific name, *sosorum*, was created in recognition of the organization's efforts.

Conservation

To protect both the salamander and the springs, in 1992 the federal government was formally requested to list the salamander as an endangered and threatened species. But the government failed to act, and the battle between the citizens of Austin, the United States Fish and Wildlife Service, and the developers continued until April 1994, when the relevant city authorities agreed on guidelines for the management of the springs. Finally, on April 30, 1997, the Barton Springs salamander was given total legal protection.

Common name Slimy salamander

Scientific name *Plethodon glutinosus*

Subfamily Plethodontinae

Family Plethodontidae

Order Caudata (Urodela)

Size 4.5 in (11 cm) to 8 in (20 cm)

Key features Body slender; legs well developed; tail is round and about the same length as the head and body combined; color black or dark gray with small sliver-white spots over all its surfaces; secretions from its tail give the skin a more slimy appearance than that of other salamanders

Habits Nocturnal; terrestrial

Breeding Fertilization is internal; females suspend clusters of 5–34 eggs from overhanging rocks and coil around them until they hatch after 2–3 months

Diet Invertebrates, especially ants and small beetles, but also a wide variety of other species

Habitat Floors of hardwood forests, swamp forests, and pine woods

Distribution Southeastern North America from Texas and Florida to New York; distribution patchy toward the south of its range

Status Common

Similar species Several other species of *Plethodon*, notably the white-spotted salamander, *P. punctatus*, and the Cumberland Plateau salamander, *P. kentucki*

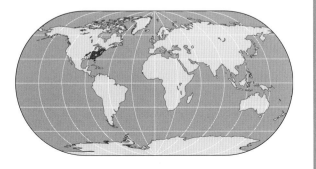

Slimy Salamander

Plethodon glutinosus

The slimy salamander lives up to both its common and scientific names. It secretes a slimy, sticky substance from glands in its tail as a defense against predators.

MANY SALAMANDERS HAVE poison glands in their skin to deter predators, but the slimy salamander is especially well endowed. Faced with a potential enemy, it raises its tail and lashes out with it. The secretions are distasteful, toxic, and may help incapacitate predators by smearing their eyes and mouth with goo. Even so, slimy salamanders fall prey to garter snakes copperheads, and probably other amphibian-eating snakes, as well as to birds, small mammals, and other salamanders.

The timing of courtship and breeding varies from one population to another. In the south it starts in February and goes on until summer, when females lay their eggs. In the north it starts in late summer or fall, and females lay the next spring or summer. Females from southern populations breed every year, but those in the north may breed only every other year.

Elaborate Courtship

The courting male goes through a sequence of maneuvers that identify him as a member of the correct species and stimulate the female to pick up his spermatophore. First, he presses his mental gland and nasolabial grooves against her head, body, or tail. Then he begins a courtship "dance," lifting and lowering his hind legs together or alternately. If he lifts them together, he uses his tail to prop up the rear of his body.

After a while he begins to raise and lower his front limbs as well, and gradually moves toward the female's head before rubbing his nasolabial grooves over her. He bites her body or tail gently, holds on for a short time, and then releases her. Next, he rubs his mental gland over the female's head and nasolabial grooves. He then pushes his head under her

SEE ALSO Snake, Common Garter **49**:84; Copperhead **50**:86

chin and walks under her, keeping in contact all the time. As his tail passes under her chin, he waves it from side to side and stops moving forward. The female steps over his tail until she is straddling it, and they move forward together, the male still waving his tail and the back part of his body. They can cover up to 15 feet (4.6 m) in this position.

When they stop, the male begins to wriggle the base of his tail from side to side, and the female follows the movement with her head. The male lowers his vent and deposits his spermatophore on the ground. They both move forward again with the female's chin in contact with the base of the male's tail until she moves over the spermatophore, which she picks up with her cloaca. This ends the sequence, and the pair go their separate ways.

When seeking females to court, males approach any other salamanders. If they happen to be other males, a fight may break out, during which they bite one another. At other times, however, the male that

⊕ *After rain showers the slimy salamander moves around the forest floor looking for invertebrate prey. If touched by human fingers, the gluelike secretions on its skin are almost impossible to remove.*

has been approached may act like a female, encouraging the courting male to deposit (and therefore waste) his spermatophore.

Smell is an important factor in identifying other salamanders of the same species, and experiments have shown that females prefer the odor of male slimy salamanders to those of related species. Scent and elaborate courtship help prevent females from mating with the wrong species and therefore laying infertile eggs. Having said that, the whole *Plethodon glutinosus* species complex seems to consist of up to 13 recognized populations, some of which interbreed, and some of which do not.

Scientists think that the species became fragmented thousands of years ago; and while some populations differentiated to the point where they no longer recognize each other as belonging to the same species, others only went part of the way down that evolutionary path. Two salamanders, the Cumberland Plateau salamander, *P. kentucki,* and the rare Tellico salamander, *P. aureolus*, have been elevated from subspecies to full species, but scientists are waiting for more information before deciding on the validity of several other proposed species.

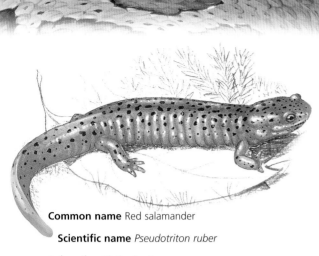

Common name Red salamander

Scientific name *Pseudotriton ruber*

Subamily Plethodontinae

Family Plethodontidae

Order Caudata (Urodela)

Size 3.8 in (9.6 cm) to 7 in (18 cm)

Key features Body stout; tail relatively short compared to many others in the family; skin appears rubbery; color varies from orange to crimson or purplish red; covered with small black spots that are more numerous on the back than the sides; juveniles more brilliantly marked than adults, which become dull with age

Habits Nocturnal; terrestrial or semiaquatic, often living in mud or under logs

Breeding Fertilization is internal; females lay clutches of 70–90 eggs that they attach to the undersides of rocks; they probably brood them until they hatch after about 12 weeks

Diet Small invertebrates and smaller salamanders

Habitat Seepages, streams, and bogs in deciduous forests and meadows

Distribution North America from southern New York to Indiana and the Gulf Coast; absent from much of the Atlantic coastal plain

Status Common in suitable habitat

Similar species The mud salamander, *Pseudotriton montanus*, is very similar but is usually orange-brown in color

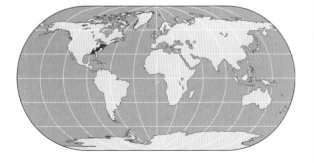

Red Salamander

Pseudotriton ruber

The red salamander is one of the most colorful salamanders in North America, although its bright coloration sometimes darkens as it ages.

THE RED COLORATION DOES not necessarily indicate that red salamanders are unpalatable: Many birds, mammals, and reptiles apparently eat them without ill effect. However, the species' range falls entirely within that of the eastern newt, *Notophthalmus viridescens*. Juveniles of that species, which are bright orange and are known as "red efts," produce powerful toxins in their skin. Therefore the red salamander might be a Batesian (harmless) mimic of the juvenile stage of the eastern newt.

Experiments show that birds learn to avoid red salamanders after they have had an unpleasant experience with red efts. Also, red salamanders defend themselves by raising their tail and coiling their body around in a manner similar to that adopted by red efts. As red efts grow to maturity, they lose their bright coloration and become brown, which might explain why adult red salamanders are not as brightly colored as juveniles.

Other research has concluded that red salamanders are Müllerian mimics because they produce some skin toxins, although they are not as strong as those of the eastern newt. (Müllerian mimics belong to a group of species that are all toxic and benefit by being similar to each other.) Other mildly toxic salamanders, such as the mud salamander, *Pseudotriton montanus*, posssibly the dusky salamander, *Desmognathus fuscus*, and other red-backed species that resemble each other (and the red salamander) superficially, may also benefit.

Simple Courtship

Compared with other plethodontids, red salamanders have a simple courtship. Males approach females and rub their snout over the

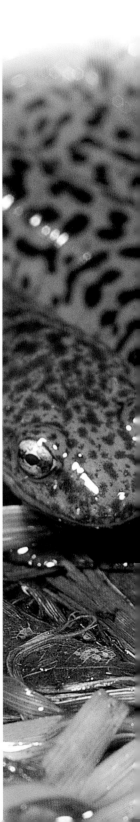

Red salamanders can be found by turning over stones or logs in or near small springs or brooks that run through woods or meadows.

female's head. Then the male forces his head under the female's chin and begins to wave his tail. She holds her chin against the base of his tail and straddles it before they walk forward for a short distance. The male then deposits his spermatophore, and the female picks it up.

Females are capable of storing sperm for very long periods after courtship, often for several months. They lay their eggs in fall or winter, selecting a shallow aquatic site such as a spring or bog through which water is continually seeping. Each egg is attached to the underside of a rock or stone by a narrow stalk and is often submerged in the water. A typical clutch consists of about 70 to 90 eggs, and the female probably stays with them, although an attended nest has not been found yet.

The eggs hatch after about three months, and the larvae make their way to slow-moving backwaters and pools where leaves and other debris collect. This provides them with somewhere to hide and is home to the large numbers of small invertebrates on which they feed. The larvae are slow growing and can take one and a half to three and a half years to metamorphose. Newly metamorphosed juveniles are relatively large and reach maturity about one year later.

Red salamanders do not seem to be territorial in the way that some related species are. They are sometimes found in large aggregations, especially in fall, when they make their way to springs and small streams to overwinter. They leave their wintering sites in the early spring and become more or less terrestrial until early summer, when they begin to gravitate back toward aquatic sites. During their terrestrial phase they live in burrows in soft mud at the side of streams or beneath logs. Red salamanders feed on a wide variety of invertebrates; but being relatively large, they can also tackle small vertebrates, especially other salamanders. Known prey items include red-backed salamanders, *Plethodon cinereus*, and frogs.

Newts and European Salamanders

The family Salamandridae is a diverse and important one, with 59 species in 15 genera. It is represented in North America (on the West Coast and over most of the eastern side of the continent), in Europe, North Africa, the Middle East, Asia, and the Far East. Its members include some of the most numerous and widespread species as well as some of the rarest. Some have been thoroughly studied, and their lives are familiar to us, while others are little known with unusual habits.

The family can be divided broadly into two groups. The first is the "salamanders." They are mainly land-dwelling species that typically return to water only to breed (although some species have dispensed with the aquatic stage in their lives altogether). They parallel the American mole salamanders, Ambystomatidae, in many ways but are restricted to the Old World, mainly Europe. Most have short tails that are roughly cylindrical in cross-section and short limbs with stubby toes. The fire salamanders, *Salamandra*, are the best examples of this type.

The second group is made up of species that are commonly called newts. They have a distinct aquatic phase, often spending several months each year in the water. Newts' tails are flattened from side to side to help in swimming. During the breeding season males of many species change color and grow fins and crests, and some also develop a degree of webbing on their feet. Newts occur in both the Old and New Worlds. The difference between the terms newts and salamanders is a loose one, based more on traditional usage than taxonomic logic.

The genus *Triturus* is the most familiar, with 12 species found across Europe and in neighboring parts of the world. As a rule, individuals live on the land for most of the year, returning to ponds and ditches in the spring to breed. In their aquatic phase males bear little

---

Common name Newts and European salamanders **Family** Salamandridae

Family Salamandridae 59 species in 15 genera (no subfamilies)

Genus *Chioglossa*—1 species, the gold-striped salamander, *C. lusitanica* from northern Portugal and northwestern Spain

Genus *Cynops*—7 species of fire-bellied newts from China and Japan, including the Japanese fire-bellied newt, *C. pyrrhogaster*

Genus *Echinotriton*—2 species of spiny newts from China and Japan

Genus *Euproctus*—3 species of brook salamanders from Europe, including the Pyrenean brook salamander, *E. asper*

Genus *Mertensiella*—1 species, the Caucasian salamander, *M. caucasica* from the Caucasus region

Genus *Neurergus*—4 species from southeastern Turkey, Iraq, and Iran

Genus *Notophthalmus*—3 species of American newts from eastern North America, including the eastern newt, or red eft, *N. viridescens*

Genus *Pachytriton*—2 species of stout newts or paddle-tailed newts from China

Genus *Paramesotriton*—5 species of warty newts from China and Vietnam

Genus *Pleurodeles*—2 species of sharp-ribbed newts from Spain, Portugal, and North Africa, including the sharp-ribbed newt, *P. waltl*

Genus *Salamandra*—6 species of salamanders from Europe, North Africa, and west Asia, including the fire salamander, *S. salamandra*

Genus *Salamandrina*—1 species, the spectacled salamander, *S. terdigitata*, from central Italy

Genus *Taricha*—3 species of rough-skinned and California newts from western North America, including *T. granulosa*

Genus *Triturus*—12 species of Old World newts from Europe, western Asia, and the Middle East, including the smooth newt, *T. vulgaris*

Genus *Tylototriton*—7 species of knobby newts, crocodile newts, or mandarin newts from China, Vietnam, Laos, and Thailand

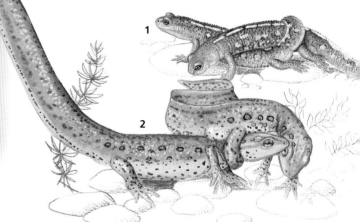

↑ *A pair of alpine newts,* Triturus alpestris, *begin courtship in a freshwater pond in Italy. The male, with its aquatic-phase colors, is on the left.*

Newts, Ewts, and Efts

In Old English the name for a newt was "ewt," or "evete." In Anglo-Saxon it was "efete." Over time efete became eft, and then ewt became a newt as the "n" moved. The word salamander is loosely translated from a Greek word meaning "fire lizard."

resemblance to their drab appearance while living on land. They develop brighter colors and often have flashes of iridescence along the flanks and the sides of their tails. Many species develop high serrated crests along their backs to improve their swimming, increase the surface area over which they can absorb oxygen, and for use in courtship displays. Some species, such as the palmate newt, *T. palmatus* from western Europe, develop partially webbed feet and thin filaments at the tip of the tail, and their eyes also change shape slightly so that they can see better under water. These species are unique in following a courtship routine in which there is no physical contact, the whole process being conducted through visual displays and chemical communication.

↩ *Courtship behavior in newts and salamanders. A male brook salamander,* Euproctus sp., *captures a female and transfers a spermatophore directly from his cloaca to hers (1); a male eastern newt,* Notophthalmus viridescens, *clasps a female's neck with his hind limbs and rubs his large cheek glands over her nostrils (2); a male red-bellied newt,* Taricha rivularis, *clasps a female from behind and rubs his chin gland over her nostrils (3); a male smooth newt,* Triturus vulgaris, *fans his tail to generate a water current that carries the odor from his skin glands to the female's nose (4).*

3

4

Many species leave the ponds immediately after the breeding season, but a few continue to be aquatic for longer, leaving only to find suitable hibernation sites on the land at the end of summer. Neoteny (retention of juvenile characteristics) occurs in several species, perhaps all, but only rarely. The fire-bellied newts, *Cynops* species from the Far East, are very similar to *Triturus* species in many respects, but males lack the extravagant crests. As their name suggests, their undersides are brightly colored, usually red but sometimes orange or yellow, warning potential predators that they are distasteful.

Skin Toxins

The American rough-skinned newts, *Taricha* from western North America, are similar to the fire-bellied newts, as are the warty newts, *Paramesotriton* from China and Vietnam, which are larger but also have bright undersides. The potency of toxins produced in the skin glands of members of both genera is well documented.

The eastern newts, *Notophthalmus* species, are common and familiar in a range of habitats. The adults are highly aquatic, with some populations staying in the water all year long, but the young are terrestrial. After metamorphosing, they go through a stage lasting two to three years when they are known as efts. Efts bear little resemblance to adults of the species, being bright orange or red to warn of skin toxins. Salamanders of other families, such as the red salamander, *Pseudotriton ruber*, may mimic the color and markings of red efts to take advantage of the fact that predators tend to avoid them.

The knobby newts, *Tylototriton*, are also from Asia. They are attractively colored with yellow or orange markings indicating where they have concentrations of poison glands in their skin. These species are somewhat intermediate in build between the land-dwelling salamanders and the aquatic newts, but many appear to be mainly aquatic, at least in captivity; their natural history is poorly known. The sharp-ribbed newts in the

genus *Pleurodeles* bear a passing resemblance to the knobby newts, having rows of orange warts along their backs that indicate poison glands, but they are duller by comparison. They defend themselves by forcing sharp ribs through their skin, releasing poison and making them painful to handle. The Chinese and Japanese spiny newts, *Echinotriton*, have gone a stage further: Their ribs are close to the surface and easily protrude through the skin if they are roughly handled. They wriggle frantically and bury their spines into anything that tries to restrain them.

Reproduction in Alpine Salamanders

The alpine salamanders, *Salamandra atra* and *S. lanzai*, and Luschan's salamander, *S. luschani*, probably have the smallest reproductive potential of any amphibian. Under the extreme conditions in which they live, they have few, if any, predators. It never gets too hot, and it never gets too dry. Their lives progress at a slow pace, since the activity period may only be a few months every year. Females breed only every two to four years and produce just two young at a time. These two young result from the first ova that are released into the oviduct and that come into contact with the stored sperm.

The remaining eggs, numbering about 20 in each oviduct, are not fertilized. Instead, they turn into a yolk mass on which the developing larvae feed. By the time the larvae are born, they are fully developed and have skipped the free-living larval stage altogether. Luschan's salamander also gives birth to two fully formed young after a gestation period lasting at least a year, but there are no available details of their development.

⊜ *The California newt,* Taricha torosa, *is one of five members of the family Salamandridae that inhabit California. It has large, bulging eyes and light-colored lower eyelids.*

⊝ *The unusual markings of this mandarin newt,* Tylototriton varrucosus *from China, provide a clue to its distasteful and potentially harmful skin toxins.*

Despite their name, the brook salamanders, *Euproctus*, are more newtlike in their behavior. They rarely leave the cool mountain rivers and streams in which they breed. They have an interesting form of amplexus in which the male holds the female with his tail. They stay like that for several days, even feeding while wrapped together. Their habitat is similar to that of many North American plethodontid salamanders that live and breed in clear, highly oxygenated water running over rocky and gravelly substrates. The three species of brook salamanders live in the Pyrenees, Corsica, and Sardinia.

The spotted newts, *Neurergus* species, are the least known. They live in the Middle East, in southeastern Turkey, Iraq, and Iran (all three species in the genus occur in Iran). Their habitat is shallow, clear mountain streams and nearby vegetation. Mating takes place near the streams, and the females lay their eggs in them. They are all at risk because of habitat destruction and pollution. Newts of the genus *Pachytriton* are from China and are fully aquatic throughout their lives. *P. labiatus* has an oar-shaped tail to help in swimming.

The remaining species in the family are largely terrestrial and are known as salamanders. The fire salamander and its relatives are the most familiar, being common throughout much of Europe and surrounding regions. They are brightly colored in shiny black and yellow. Previously regarded as one widespread species with many subspecies, they are now divided into five species. One of them, the European fire salamander, *Salamandra salamandra*, still has a number of distinct races or subspecies.

The jet-black alpine salamanders, of which there are two species, *S. atra* and *S. lanzai*, live at altitudes up to 10,000 feet (3,000 m) in the Alps of southwestern Europe, where their habitat is often dripping with mist and very cold, even in the summer. Luschan's salamander, *S. luschani*, which is brown with irregular yellow or orange markings, occurs in just a small area of southwestern Turkey and on a handful of small Adriatic islands.

Luschan's salamander was placed until recently in the genus *Mertensiella*, which now has only a single member. It is the Caucasian salamander, *M. caucasica*. It has a long tail and is patterned with yellow dots on a darker background color. Males of this species and

Unken Reflex

The term "Unken reflex" comes from the German word *Unke*. The word is taken from the noise made by the little fire-bellied toad, *Bombina bombina*, that lives in northern Europe. Fire-bellied toads have a well-known defensive behavior in which they arch their backs and display the bright-red areas under their body and limbs. Many newts and salamanders have a similar strategy. Since many of them are red, orange, or yellow underneath, they need a mechanism for showing off the colors if they feel threatened. They do this by raising their tail and head, sometimes waving the tail from side to side or forming it into a coil. The crested newt, *Triturus cristatus*, may also tilt its body to display the bright-orange underside, and the American western newts, *Taricha*, arch their backs until nearly all their undersides are on show, sometimes flipping over in the process.

⊖ *Defensive postures. The spiny newt, Echinotriton andersoni (1), and the red-bellied newt, Taricha rivularis (5), use the Unken reflex; the ensatina, Ensatina eschscholtzii, lashes out with its tail (3); the cave salamander waves its tail from side to side (2); the mole salamander, Ambystoma talpoideum, head-butts (4).*

SEE ALSO Fire-Bellied Toads **42**:24

Luschan's salamander
have fleshy "spines" on top
of their tails that they apparently use to
stimulate the female's cloaca during amplexus. The
Caucasian salamander is more prolific than Luschan's,
producing 10 to 20 eggs in a single clutch each year. The
emergent larvae live in streams for up to three years
before metamorphosing.

Two other European salamanders belong to genera
with a single species each. The gold-striped salamander,
Chioglossa lusitanica, grows to about 6 inches (15 cm),
two-thirds of which consists of the tail. The tail, however,
is sometimes shorter as a result of having been shed as a
defense mechanism and then regrown. The technique is
more commonly associated with lungless salamanders
(family Plethodontidae), with which it also shares the
ability to shoot out its tongue to catch insects. It occurs in
northwestern Spain and northern Portugal, living

⊕ *The gold-striped salamander,*
Chioglossa lusitanica *from Spain, can shed its tail as a defensive*
measure. Its tail accounts for up to two-thirds of its total body length
and serves as an area for storing fat.

alongside mountain streams in cool valleys. The
spectacled salamander, *Salamandrina terdigitata*, lives in
Italy, favoring shady, wooded mountain slopes near
streams in the western Apennines. It grows only to
4 inches (10 cm) and is black on top with a white mark
joining its eyes, hence its common name. It is bright red
under its tail and limbs, and has mottled black-and-white
coloring under its body. It is a very secretive animal and
seems to disappear from the surface for much of the year.

Common name Japanese fire-bellied newt

Scientific name *Cynops pyrrhogaster*

Family Salamandridae

Order Caudata (Urodela)

Size 3.5 in (9 cm) to 4.5 in (11 cm)

Key features Typical newt with a long, flattened tail and 4 well-developed limbs; skin rough; raised parotid gland immediately behind the head; irregular raised ridge along each side of back; color dark chocolate-brown or black, with bright red or orange (occasionally yellow) underside; underside mottled or spotted with the same color as the back

Habits Adults aquatic for most of the year but terrestrial in warm weather

Breeding Fertilization is internal; females attach their eggs to aquatic plants; clutch size may total 324; eggs hatch after about 3 weeks

Diet Invertebrates such as small worms and insects, and their larvae

Habitat Streams and pools in humid regions

Distribution Japan (Honshu, Shikoku, and Kyushu Islands)

Status Common

Similar species Japanese sword-tailed newt, *Cynops ensicauda*, is larger and has white markings on its flanks; 5 other species of fire-bellied newts also live in China

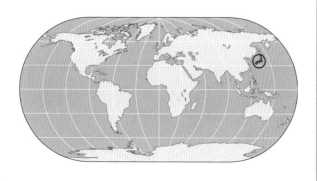

Japanese Fire-Bellied Newt

Cynops pyrrhogaster

The bright underside of the Japanese fire-bellied newt warns predators that it is unpalatable. The unpleasant taste is caused by substances produced in glands in its skin, especially behind the head and along its back.

THE JAPANESE FIRE-BELLIED NEWT successfully combines camouflage with warning coloration. When seen from above (from a bird's viewpoint, for example), its dark dorsal coloration blends in with the rocky or muddy bottom of the pools, paddy fields, or sluggish streams in which it lives. From below, however (where it may be seen by a predatory fish), its brilliant underside warns of the potent toxins produced in its glands. The newt has an additional defensive tactic: It reacts to an enemy by raising its chin and its tail, displaying its bright underside.

Variation among Forms

Japanese fire-bellied newts come from three separate islands, and there is variation among the populations. The "sasayamae" form, for example, has small pearly-white spots within the dark areas on its underside, while other forms have solid orange undersides with few or no dark spots. Males from the Atsumi Peninsula have a fine filament, or thread, extending from the end of their tail.

Differences also extend to their habits, with some forms being almost entirely aquatic throughout the year, while some enter water to breed but return to land as soon as the breeding season ends. Others are intermediate: They spend most of their time in the water but emerge to live on land during warm weather, probably to escape the excessive heat by sheltering under rocks and logs.

Juveniles of all forms usually emerge onto the land once they have metamorphosed. They live a terrestrial life until they reach sexual maturity at the age of two or three years.

⬆ *It is only from beneath that an observer gets the full benefit of the Japanese fire-bellied newt's vivid colors. Seen from above, it is dark and inconspicuous.*

Oriental Relatives

There are seven species in the genus *Cynops* (including *C. pyrrhogaster*), and they all have brightly colored undersides. One species, the larger sword-tailed newt, *C. ensicauda*, also comes from Japan, but farther south on the island groups of Oshima and Okinawa (Ryuku Islands). The other five species are (or were) Chinese. The Chinese fire-bellied newt, *C. orientalis*, has the largest range of any species in the genus and lives over most of eastern China. It is a small species with a less warty skin than *C. pyrrhogaster*, and its belly is plain red. It is often seen in the pet trade (and is sometimes incorrectly labeled as *C. pyrrhogaster*). The other four species have very small ranges and are all rare. The Kunming Lake fire-bellied newt, *Cynops wolterstorffi*, is probably extinct as a result of habitat degradation. In the 1950s it was very abundant in Kunming Lake, Yunnan, with thousands of individuals observed in the breeding season. However, since 1979 none has been found, but there is one report of a fisherman seeing one individual in 1984.

Breeding

Females start to form eggs when the water temperature reaches 68°F (20°C), and courtship tales place in the water. Males develop swollen cloacae, smoother skin, and a flattened tail, sometimes with a purple sheen and ending in a fine filament. The male approaches a female and butts her flanks with his head. He rubs her body with his parotid glands and uses his tail to fan water containing his pheromones toward her. Other males are chased away aggressively. Males of some populations place one or more feet on the female's body while they are displaying. The female responds by nudging the male's cloaca, and he deposits a spermatophore. He leads her forward until her cloaca is over the spermatophore, and she picks it up.

One or two days later the female begins to lay between one and 16 eggs a day for up to 50 days until she has laid a full complement, which can total as many as 324. She attaches each one individually to the leaf axil of an aquatic plant, folding the leaf over it with her hind feet to prevent it from being found and eaten by other newts. The eggs hatch after about three weeks, and the larvae feed on tiny aquatic crustaceans. They metamorphose in two to four months. Japanese fire-bellied newts have lived for up to 25 years in captivity.

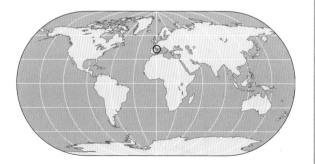

Common name Pyrenean brook salamander

Scientific name *Euproctus asper*

Family Salamandridae

Order Caudata (Urodela)

Size 6 in (15 cm)

Key features Body stout; head flat; eyes small; neck has no glands; skin is covered with many small, horny-tipped warts; tail flattened and accounts for about half the total length, slightly longer in males than in females; color olive-brown, gray, or brown, often with dirty yellow spots and stripes; yellow stripe sometimes runs along the dorsal midline, especially in juveniles

Habits Mainly aquatic; nocturnal

Breeding Fertilization is internal; female lays 20–40 eggs and places them in crevices or attaches them to stones; eggs hatch after about 6 weeks

Diet Aquatic invertebrates

Habitat Mountain streams and cool lakes at high altitudes

Distribution Pyrenees Mountains on the border of Spain and France

Status Common in suitable habitat

Similar species The sharp-ribbed newt, *Pleurodeles waltl*, is similar in color but does not live in the Pyrenees; 2 other brook salamanders, *E. montanus* and *E. platycephalus*, live on Corsica and Sardinia respectively

Pyrenean Brook Salamander

Euproctus asper

The Pyrenean brook salamander is an unusual newt that lives in the cold mountain streams flowing down the slopes of the Spanish and French Pyrenees.

ALTHOUGH COOL, HIGHLY oxygenated streams are often home to salamanders in North America (especially those in the family Plethodontidae), this type of habitat is not much used by salamanders and newts in other parts of the world. However, the Pyrenean brook salamander's lungs are small. Therefore, like the plethodontid salamanders, it relies heavily on respiration through its skin.

It lives at between 2,100 and 7,500 feet (640–2,300 m), where the temperature of slow-flowing stretches of rivers and streams rarely rises over 59°F (15°C), and where the bottom is covered in stones and boulders. At lower altitudes it spends most of its time in the water, but it can live on land and is sometimes found under rocks at the water's edge. If its aquatic habitat dries up, it estivates on land. At higher altitudes it hibernates on land for up to eight months while the streams and lakes are covered in ice and snow.

Caught in His Tail

Courtship and mating take place in water. The Pyrenean brook salamander and two closely related European species, the Corsican brook salamander, *E. montanus*, and the Sardinian brook salamander, *E. platycephalus*, have a unique courtship in which males use their tails to restrain the females. On seeing a female, the male raises himself onto the tips of his toes and lifts his tail, displaying the bright orange or red along its underside. As soon as the female approaches, the male captures her with his tail and wraps it around her lower abdomen. They may remain in this position for several hours before the male maneuvers their bodies to press their cloacae together. He then transfers his

⊕ *In the Pyrenees Mountains in France a male Pyrenean brook salamander wraps his tail around a female during mating.*

spermatophore directly into the female. The Corsican and Sardinian species also use their jaws and hind limbs to restrain the female, and may use their hind limbs to place the spermatophore into the female's cloaca.

Courtship and spermatophore transfer take place in the fall, but the female stores the sperm until the following spring, when she lays 20 to 40 eggs. Using her protrusible cloaca, she pushes them into crevices and under rocks. The eggs hatch about six weeks later, and the larvae usually spend at least one winter as larvae before they metamorphose. They reach sexual maturity at two to fours years, depending on the altitude and therefore the temperature at which they live. Pyrenean brook salamanders have lived for 26 years in captivity.

Direct transfer of the spermatophore from the male to the female has several advantages for the brook salamanders. First, it prevents

Island Relatives

There are only three members in the genus *Euproctus*. Scientists think that their ancestors once lived over much of Europe but had to retreat during a period of glaciation. Subsequently they became isolated on a mountain range and two islands. The island species (*E. montanus* from Corsica and *E. platycephalus* from Sardinia) are slightly smaller than the Pyrenean brook salamander and have smoother skin. Courtship is similar, but the Sardinian brook salamander lays up to 220 eggs, far more than the other two species. It is listed as Critically Endangered by the IUCN due to its small, fragmented range, which appears to be shrinking.

other males from stealing the female after the male has attracted her. Second, it avoids the possibility of his spermatophore being washed away in the flowing water. Furthermore, unlike other newts that breed in water, the male may not be able to waft pheromones toward the female using his tail as a fan. Stream-dwelling plethodontids in North America usually carry out their courtship on land.

Red eft stage

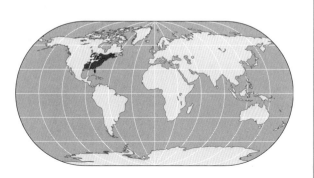

Common name Eastern newt (red-spotted newt)

Scientific name *Notophthalmus viridescens*

Family Salamandridae

Order Caudata (Urodela)

Size 2.5 in (6.3 cm) to 4.5 in (11 cm)

Key features Small newt with velvety skin; tail accounts for about half the total length and has a narrow keel above and below; adults are olive above and yellow below with both surfaces speckled with tiny black flecks; row of small, round, bright-red spots bordered with black on each side, sometimes joined together to form broken stripes; juveniles bright to dull orange

Habits Aquatic, semiaquatic, and terrestrial depending on stage of life and other factors

Breeding Fertilization is internal; females lay eggs singly over a long period; total eggs laid can number 25–350; eggs hatch after 20–35 days

Diet Small invertebrates on the land and in water

Habitat Permanent and semipermanent ponds, lakes, reservoirs, ditches, and swamps in forests or open farmland

Distribution Eastern North America

Status Very common

Similar species 2 other species of *Notophthalmus* are similar but lack the small red markings

Eastern Newt

Notophthalmus viridescens

The eastern newt is found in quiet pools or backwaters of rivers in forests or in meadows. Juvenile red efts can be seen during the day near woodlands after rain.

THE EASTERN NEWT TYPICALLY goes through three stages: It begins life as an aquatic larva, metamorphoses to become a terrestrial juvenile (known as an eft), and then develops into an aquatic adult. To further complicate a confusing sequence of events, there is great variation.

Some individuals skip the intermediate terrestrial juvenile stage and remain in the water after they have metamorphosed into aquatic juveniles. Others reach adulthood without having metamorphosed completely, so they become neotenous adults with external gills. Adults may return to the water after they have matured and stay there for the rest of their lives. Alternatively, they may remain there as long as possible but leave temporarily if the ponds begin to dry up or become overheated; or they may simply return to the water and breed, leaving once the breeding season is over. Some, but not all, of this variation is related to locality, although some populations include individuals that have different life cycles.

Red Efts

The most familiar form is probably the red eft. It is a small, bright- to dull-orange newt that lives among leaf litter. Red efts are more likely to be active in the day than other amphibians because they gain some protection through the bright coloration that warns of poisonous secretions from glands in their skin. Red efts are ten times as toxic as adult eastern newts and are avoided by many predators, including American toads, garter snakes, red-tailed hawks, and raccoons. Their defense is not as effective against nocturnal hunters (because the bright colors are not easily visible), and bullfrogs and some turtles will eat them. There is a record of a hognose snake eating one and another of a Boy Scout in New York State in the 1940s

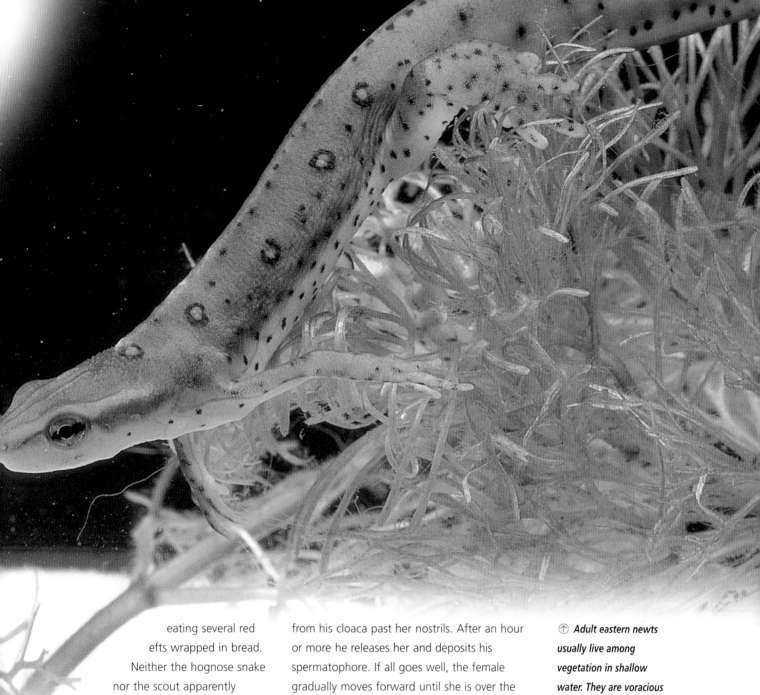

Adult eastern newts usually live among vegetation in shallow water. They are voracious feeders, preying on worms, insects, small crustaceans and mollusks, as well as amphibian eggs and larvae.

eating several red efts wrapped in bread. Neither the hognose snake nor the scout apparently suffered any ill effects!

Breeding

Courtship in eastern newts is variable. At its simplest the male displays in front of the female, she nudges his tail, he drops his spermatophore, and she picks it up in her cloaca. This occurs in less than 30 percent of encounters. In the others the male has to work harder to stimulate the female, and courtship involves a form of amplexus—the male grasps the female just behind her front limbs with his hind limbs. At the same time, he rubs her snout with his front limbs and the sides of his head. He curls his tail around and wafts secretions from his cloaca past her nostrils. After an hour or more he releases her and deposits his spermatophore. If all goes well, the female gradually moves forward until she is over the spermatophore and picks it up. Unfortunately, in just over half the encounters the female swims away without picking it up. In other cases another male darts between the male and female at the last minute and deposits his own spermatophore, sometimes eating that of the first male. Surprisingly, females are as likely to pick up the cheater's spermatophore as that of their courtship partner.

Females lay their eggs singly, attaching each one to the leaf of an aquatic plant and carefully folding the leaf over it with their hind legs. Since they lay only a few eggs each day, and they can total 25 to 350, egg laying can take several weeks to complete.

Common name Sharp-ribbed newt (Spanish sharp-ribbed newt)

Scientific name *Pleurodeles waltl*

Family Salamandridae

Order Caudata (Urodela)

Size 6 in (15 cm) to 12 in (30 cm)

Key features Stocky newt; face resembles a toad—flattened, rounded, warty, with small eyes on top; entire body is covered with small granules, each with a black horny tip; a row of larger orange poison glands runs down each flank, marking the ends of its ribs; tail accounts for about half its total length and is flattened from side to side

Habits Highly aquatic but sometimes migrates across land if its habitat dries up

Breeding Fertilization is internal; females lay large numbers of eggs, scattering them over a wide area; eggs hatch after 5–14 days

Diet Invertebrates, including tadpoles, and small vertebrates

Habitat Almost any lowland body of water, including ponds, ditches, wells, sluggish rivers, and streams, especially if choked with vegetation

Distribution Spain and Portugal, except the north, and the coastal plain of northern Morocco

Status Very common

Similar species The related *Pleurodeles poireti* lives in northern Algeria and northern Tunisia

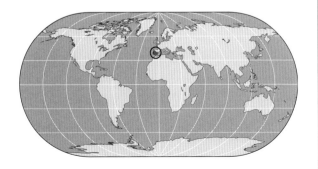

Sharp-Ribbed Newt

Pleurodeles waltl

The sharp-ribbed newt is unlike any other newt except a closely related North African species. It has unique defensive tactics, unusual courtship, and the sex of its offspring is determined by the water temperature.

THE SHARP-RIBBED NEWT is one of the largest tailed amphibians in Europe. It is tough, voracious, and pugnacious, and it eats anything it can catch. It can live in almost any body of water, including stagnant pools, but prefers weed-choked ponds and ditches. It usually stays hidden in the mud near the bottom and only comes to the surface to breathe. If its pond dries up or becomes overheated in the summer, it will retreat to the land and shelter under rocks, logs, or piles of dead vegetation, surviving even in dry conditions for a while. Very occasionally it will travel across the land in search of a new pond.

It feeds in the water, taking invertebrates such as worms and insect larvae, fish, tadpoles, and even smaller individuals of its own species. It has a remarkable capacity for food—a captive sharp-ribbed newt was seen wrestling with an earthworm three times its length and half its weight. A few minutes later it was cruising the bottom of its aquarium looking for more! Not surprisingly, it grows rapidly and can reach sexual maturity within a year of metamorphosis.

Ribs as Weapons

The sharp-ribbed newt is prepared to bite if attacked and will sometimes give off a defensive yelping sound. Its main lines of defense, however, are its ribs. They are sharply pointed, and their tips are positioned just beneath the surface of the skin, coinciding with the position of seven to 10 dull orange warts down each side of its back. They are poison glands. If the salamander feels under threat, it arches its back. The action pulls the skin tight over the ends of the ribs, which pierce the skin through the poison glands, releasing toxins onto its surface. If the newt is seized, however, it writhes around vigorously, forcing the ribs through its skin, and it may also pinch the predator between two of its projecting ribs. Individuals that have used this method of defense in the past sometimes have the ends of their ribs projecting permanently from their back, the skin having healed around them. The Chinese and Japanese spiny newts, *Echinotriton*, have a similar mechanism.

Courtship and breeding

The sharp-ribbed newt breeds throughout the year if conditions are right, often in response to rain, but generally between September and March. Males develop rough black patches of skin on the insides of their front limbs when they are in breeding condition. During courtship the male approaches the female from behind and below, and nudges her with his snout. He moves under her body and rubs her throat with the top of his head, at the same time looping his front limbs around hers while holding her with his tail.

The whole process can take up to one hour; and once amplexus has been achieved, they can remain in this position for several more hours before the spermatophore transfer takes place. Even then, the male may stay in position until the female starts to lay eggs, presumably to guard against other males taking his place. The female lays the eggs several days later, attaching 150 to 800 (exceptionally as many as 2,000) eggs to stones or plants in groups of nine to 20. Eggs are laid over a long period, sometimes up to a month. The eggs hatch after five to 14 days, and the larvae metamorphose in 50 to 150 days depending on temperature. The young sometimes leave the water and live under stones around the edge of the pond.

⬇ *The orange patches on the side of its body correspond to the "sharp ribs" from which* Pleurodeles waltl *gets its common name. The ribs pierce the skin through the poison glands located beneath the orange spots and can deliver a toxic stab to a predator.*

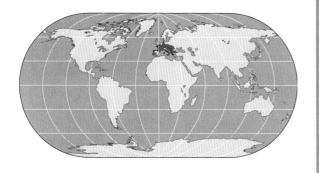

Common name Fire salamander

Scientific name *Salamandra salamandra*

Family Salamandridae

Order Caudata (Urodela)

Size 7 in (18 cm) to 11 in (28 cm)

Key features Body chunky; tail short and round in cross-section; limbs stocky; toes stumpy; head wide; skin rubbery both in appearance and in feel; most forms are glossy jet black with markings of various shapes, usually bright yellow but occasionally red or orange; in some forms the yellow markings almost or completely cover the body

Habits Secretive and nocturnal but sometimes active in the day during rainy or misty weather

Breeding Variable; mating takes place on the land; the female usually gives birth to aquatic larvae, but some forms give birth to live juveniles; gestation period very variable

Diet Insects and worms

Habitat Forests of all kinds, usually in hilly or mountainous regions; lightly wooded valleys with streams; rarely found in and around montane lakes

Distribution Europe, with closely related species in North Africa and western Asia

Status Locally common

Similar species Other members of the genus can resemble certain forms, but there is no overlap between species

Fire Salamander *Salamandra salamandra*

The original, mythical salamander was a legendary beast that could survive in, and even extinguish, fires. The Roman author Pliny and the Greek philosopher Aristotle wrote about the supernatural powers of the salamander.

STORIES OF THE SALAMANDER'S ability to withstand burning probably arose because a salamander's skin is always cold to the touch, and because it secretes a fluid from pores in its body if it is annoyed. This may have been construed as an attempt to put out fire. Its association with fire comes from its habit of hiding in dead and rotting wood, which may have been collected for firewood. During the winter when the wood was put on the fire, the salamander would have woken up and escaped. To superstitious people this would have been a sign that the animal had supernatural powers.

Other folk stories tell of a material, supposedly woven with "salamander wool" that could be worn to protect against fire. In reality it was asbestos. Nowadays companies making fire-related products such as stoves and incinerators sometimes use "salamander" as a trade or brand name.

Forest Habitat

Fire salamanders are found across Europe, mostly in damp, well-wooded hilly or mountainous countryside with a deep layer of leaf litter and plenty of rocks to hide under. Slow-moving streams are usually required for breeding, but some forms get around the problem by giving birth to fully formed young.

Fire salamanders can occur in very high densities. A short walk with a flashlight in good salamander habitat often reveals dozens of individuals dotted around the forest floor, while a drive along a quiet forest road will be punctuated by a fire salamander every few

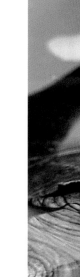

⊕ **Salamandra salamandra** *in a pond in Germany. Although adult fire salamanders seek out water for breeding purposes, they cannot swim.*

yards. A night of drizzle or light rain gets salamanders moving in especially large numbers. During the day or in dry weather, however, there will be no sign of them.

Fire salamander populations vary in the amount of yellow on their bodies and the shape of their markings. The variation reflects their history as a species. The Pleistocene period marked the beginning of four glaciations, the last of which finally receded about 10,000 years ago. At their greatest extent ice sheets covered most of northern Europe, and the only regions that were mild enough to be inhabited by salamanders were the Iberian, Italian, and Balkan peninsulas. Fire salamanders living on these peninsulas were isolated from the others and evolved different characteristics, notably their markings, but also size, shape, and behavior. As the ice sheets moved north, the salamander populations were able to spread out, and some came into contact with each other. In central Germany, for example, the

Meet the Relatives

Until recently the genus *Salamandra* had just two species—the fire salamander, *S. salamandra,* and the alpine salamander, *S. atra.* Recent reclassification has split the fire salamanders into four species and the alpine salamanders into two. In addition, Luschan's salamander, *S. luschani,* which used to belong to the genus *Mertensiella,* is now placed in the genus *Salamandra.* The species now are:

S. salamandra—the familiar fire salamander found throughout most of Europe

S. algira—North African fire salamander

S. corsica—Corsican fire salamander

S. infraimmaculata—Middle Eastern fire salamander from Israel, Turkey, and Lebanon

S.atra—alpine salamander; totally jet-black species from the Alps of Switzerland, southern Germany, Austria, northern Italy, Slovenia, and Croatia; *S. atra aurorae,* the form from northeastern Italy, has a large area of white, gray, or yellow down the middle of its back

S. lanzai—Lanza's alpine salamander; similar to the alpine salamander, but larger with a more flattened head; lives in the Cottian Alps (northwestern Italy) and adjacent parts of France

S. luschani—Luschan's salamander; a small species that occurs only in extreme southwestern Turkey and on a few islands off the Turkish coast

↥ *Fire salamander subspecies display a variety of forms and coloring. The overall bright-yellow* Salamandra salamandra giglioli *is a subspecies from southern Italy.*

western striped form and the eastern spotted form meet. In areas where their ranges overlap, their body markings are intermediate— broken stripes and spots are randomly scattered over their backs. Other populations have remained isolated, however, and form distinct races or subspecies, often where mountain ranges are surrounded by areas of unsuitable habitat or on islands. Scientists debate which of them are worthy of subspecies status and which should be regarded as full species. In 2000 several forms were elevated to full species.

In addition to geographical races there is variation within races. In particular, some forms have a proportion of individuals in which the markings are red or orange instead of yellow. Spotted fire salamanders from northern Portugal, *S. s. gallaica*, seem most likely to show this variation, but it also crops up occasionally in others. In some races the black markings are reduced, and fire salamanders from southern Italy, subspecies *S. s. giglioli*, are sometimes completely yellow.

Defensive Males
Fire salamanders start to breed when they are three or four years old, with females usually taking longer than males to reach sexual maturity. The breeding season varies according to location but typically occurs in the fall. Males are territorial, and on wet nights during the breeding season they position themselves on prominent landmarks such as stumps, exposed roots, or small piles of stones. They defend their territory against other males by chasing them, straddling the other male's back, or by grappling with its front legs. The older male usually wins these bouts.

Courtship takes place entirely on land. The male nudges the female's flanks and head

before forcing his way underneath her body and looping his front limbs over hers from below. He deposits his spermatophore on the ground, usually on a flat surface, then swivels sideways about 45 degrees to allow the female to lower her cloaca to the ground and pick up the spermatophore. Females can store sperm for up to two and a half years, but a fall mating usually results in egg fertilization the following spring. When the female ovulates, the sperm moves up into her oviduct to fertilize the eggs, and they begin to develop in the oviduct.

Birthing Options
The developing embryos are held in the female's oviduct for a varying length of time— up to one year in some cases. Typically, she gives birth to late-stage larvae by reversing into shallow water so that they can swim away to continue their development in the normal way. However, sometimes she retains them until they have metamorphosed, in which case she gives birth to fully formed juveniles.

Which strategy she uses depends largely on geography: Fire salamanders from northern Spain, *S. s. bernerdezi*, are usually live-bearers. There is some flexibility, however, and the Pyrenean form, *S. s. fastuosa*, may also give birth to live young under certain circumstances, while the northern Spanish ones may also start life as larvae in some circumstances. Factors that affect the "choice" include altitude and rainfall—mountainous forms and species from drier regions are more likely to give birth to fully formed live young.

Where they occur, aquatic larvae are of the pond type with high dorsal and caudal fins and large external gills. They are usually deposited in streams and may accumulate in slow-moving sections so that they do not get swept away. In some places roadside troughs (installed for the benefit of packhorses in the past) are fed by mountain streams and often contain

→ *Also known as the yellow-striped fire salamander, the Pyrenean form,* Salamandra s. fastuosa, *occurs in mountain habitats in northern Spain.*

salamander larvae, presumably born upstream and washed into them.

The larvae feed on small aquatic invertebrates, eating whatever is most common. In places cannibalism can occur if larvae of different sizes live together. As they grow, mottled markings appear on their bodies; and by the time they metamorphose, they have traces of the adult pattern. Full adult black-and-yellow coloration does not develop for several months, however.

Squirting Poison

Fire salamanders are extremely toxic. Their secretions will easily kill a dog and possibly a human, which is why they are so brightly colored. They have large poison glands behind each eye (parotid glands), and the pores through which the milky, sticky poison is forced are easily visible. There are two additional rows of poison glands along the salamander's back. It can squirt the poison from the glands up to 6 feet (1.8 m) by contracting the muscles that surround them, tilting its body so that the streams of fluid are aimed at the predator. It is an effective and unusual response; most other salamanders can only release poison when the predator bites or squeezes them.

A very similar arrangement of skin glands occurs in the alpine salamander, *S. atra*, and in Luschan's salamander, *S. luschani*. These species can probably also spray their secretions. The toxins belong to a group of chemicals known as alkaloids, which cause muscle convulsions. In addition to repelling predators, the toxins may also act as broad-based antibiotics, protecting the salamander's sensitive skin against attack by fungi and bacteria.

Lifestyle and Feeding

Fire salamanders are usually nocturnal, but they are sometimes active on the surface on dull, rainy days. Otherwise they spend their days hiding under logs, in leaf litter, or in burrows in thick moss. Unlike the American mole salamanders, which resemble them to some extent, they do not dig their own burrows.

Their eyes are adapted to see in dim light, having more rod cells than cone cells in the retina (rods are more sensitive to dim light). The larvae also avoid bright conditions and hide under stones and dead leaves during the day.

Adult salamanders may wander up to 30 yards (27 m) from their daytime retreat in the course of a night but always find their way back to the same place. Even if they are moved experimentally, they have a good homing instinct as long as they are released in a familiar area, but they easily become disoriented in total darkness. Their sense of smell is probably not as important as sight. This fact is also borne out in their hunting habits, since they tend to examine potential food by sight. When there is some light, food needs to be moving to attract their attention; but in darkness they will eat stationary prey, even though they have trouble

⊖ *Fire salamanders prey on whatever is available locally, but mainly insects and other invertebrates. Here* Salamandra salamandra *tackles an earthworm.*

finding it. In other words, they use their sense of smell when they have to, but it is inferior to their sight.

They eat a wide variety of prey, but there is some variation among populations and also among individuals. The central Spanish fire salamander, *S. s. almanzoris*, lives around high montane lakes where there are no earthworms, so it feeds mainly on beetles, their larvae, and flies. In the Pyrenees, on the other hand, the Pyrenean fire salamander, *S. s. fastuosa*, favors earthworms, and some will eat nothing else. Both larvae and young adults eat whatever is most common in their habitat, and in experiments newly metamorphosed young were able to be imprinted so that even as adults they tended to favor prey that they had encountered during the first few weeks of their lives. In captivity salamanders caught in the wild can sometimes be difficult to feed with easily available items, but captive-bred salamanders that have been raised on a certain diet continue to be easily catered to.

Fire Salamanders of Mount Carmel

Fire salamanders on Mount Carmel in northern Israel were studied for a period of over 15 years. It was found that this population has adapted to harsh conditions in several unusual ways. These fire salamanders now belong to the species *Salamandra infraimmaculata*, but at the time of the research they were still classified as *S. salamandra*.

The habitat in that part of the world is dry, and the salamanders are restricted to the northern portion of the mountain range, where the rainfall is highest. However, the total adult population may be only between 100 and 200 animals, and they live at a low density of one salamander every 240 to 360 square yards (200–300 sq. m). They are larger on average than salamanders from other populations, which helps them avoid dehydration. That is because large bodies have a smaller surface area relative to weight compared to small ones, and therefore there is relatively less evaporation.

Their breeding cycle is also adaptive. Some females breed in November, but others wait until December. If the year is a dry one, the November batch of larvae die because the ponds dry up, but the December larvae survive because the December rains fill up the ponds again. If the year is a wet one, however, the November larvae will already have grown when the December larvae are deposited, and the early larvae cannibalize the later ones. Wet years occur every three or four years. Females that "bet" on wet years and lay in November will lose all of their offspring most of the time; but when there is plenty of rain, their offspring hit the jackpot because they have a plentiful and high-quality food supply. Therefore, when they metamorphose, they are larger than average and have a better chance of surviving to adulthood.

Common name Rough-skinned newt

Scientific name *Taricha granulosa*

Family Salamandridae

Order Caudata (Urodela)

Size 6.1 in (15.5 cm) to 8.6 in (22 cm)

Key features Heavily built newt; skin rough due to its covering of small warts; color dark brown or black with an orange or yellow underside, sometimes with a few dark markings

Habits Adults and juveniles terrestrial; larvae aquatic; adults secretive, emerging at night to feed

Breeding Fertilization is internal and follows courtship in which amplexus takes place; female lays eggs that she attaches singly to aquatic plants or debris

Diet Small invertebrates, such as insects and worms; frogs' eggs and tadpoles

Habitat Damp forests, sometimes fields and meadows, in hilly or mountainous countryside; larvae live in temporary or permanent ponds, lakes, and ditches

Distribution Western North America from southeastern Alaska to San Francisco Bay but not extending far inland

Status Common

Similar species 2 related species, the red-bellied newt, *Taricha rivularis*, and the California newt, *T. torosa*, live in the same region; they are all very similar, but *T. rivularis* has a rich red underside (the others have orange bellies), and *T. torosa* has larger eyes; distinguishing the latter species from *T. granulosa* in places where they both occur is difficult

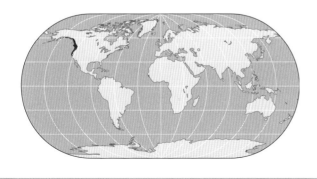

Rough-Skinned Newt

Taricha granulosa

The skin of the rough-skinned newt contains powerful poisons—easily enough to kill or repel a potential predator. The toxins are even capable of killing a human foolhardy enough to eat one.

THE ROUGH-SKINNED NEWT is far more toxic than the two other species of *Taricha* (*T. rivularis*, the red-bellied newt, and *T. torosa*, the California newt), but the eggs of all three species are equally toxic. In experiments an amount of preparation from its skin too small to visualize killed a laboratory mouse in under 10 minutes. Surprisingly, however, one of its main predators, the red-spotted garter snake, *Thamnophis sirtalis concinnus*, seems to be immune to its effects, while other species of garter snakes become paralyzed. On Vancouver Island the newts are less toxic than elsewhere, and the garter snakes there are less resistant to the newt toxin.

As a second means of defense, rough-skinned newts arch their backs, close their eyes, and raise their tail and head to reveal their bright undersides in a warning display.

Locating Breeding Ponds

In the spring adult rough-skinned newts make their way to breeding ponds, which may be temporary pools, beaver ponds, or larger bodies of water. However, the timing can vary from place to place—at high altitudes breeding may not take place until October, while nearer the coast they breed from January to April. The newts move mostly at night and especially during wet weather.

Several experiments have been conducted to test the species' homing instinct. Results have shown that animals that are moved over 500 yards (450 m) from their home ranges always return, sometimes in less than 12 hours. They seem to orient themselves using scent and celestial cues, and they may also use memory.

 SEE ALSO Snake, Common Garter 49:84

Many move along small streams until they arrive at the breeding pools.

Most females breed every year, but some breed every second year. There is also regional variation in their behavior after breeding: In some places they leave the water once egg laying is finished, but in others they stay for the remainder of the year, leaving only in the fall to find somewhere to hibernate. In California adults usually remain in the water throughout the year unless heavy rain washes them out. Even during the breeding season individual newts may leave the pond temporarily, perhaps to search for food.

Courtship consists of a dorsal amplexus in which the male grasps the female just behind her front

Mysterious Gatherings

For reasons that are not fully understood, rough-skinned newts sometimes come together to form large aggregations. One contained about 5,000 males and females that had recently bred. They were in the channel of a reservoir, and covered an area of about 22 square yards (18 sq. m). They gradually dispersed over the next few weeks, probably to their overwintering sites.

Another record involved a group of 259 newts, including large larvae, juveniles, and adults grouped together under objects along the shore of Crater Lake, Oregon. Newts from Crater Lake are unusual in having dark blotches on their bellies, and they are considered to be a distinct subspecies, *T. granulosa mazamae.*

⊕ Amplexus in rough-skinned newts can last for up to two days. Should they need to come to the surface to breathe during this time, they do so still locked together.

limbs and just in front of her hind limbs. While in this position, he uses his chin and his hind limbs to stroke various parts of the female's body. They can remain coupled like this for up to two days until the female raises her head, presumably to signal that she is ready to pick up a spermatophore. The male releases his grip and moves around to the front of the female. She places her snout in contact with his cloaca. After depositing the spermatophore, he swings his body around, while the female keeps her snout in contact with his cloaca. Eventually, she will be positioned directly over the spermatophore, which she picks up with her cloaca. At this point the male may go back into amplexus again, and the process may be repeated several times.

The female begins egg laying shortly after mating and attaches the eggs singly to aquatic plants or underwater debris. The larvae usually grow to metamorphosis by the end of the summer, but at high elevations they overwinter and transform the following year.

Common name Smooth newt (common newt)

Scientific name *Triturus vulgaris*

Family Salamandridae

Order Caudata (Urodela)

Size 4.5 in (11 cm)

Key features Small newt; skin smooth and slightly velvety when seen on land; color yellowish brown with small black flecks on the back; in the breeding season males develop larger black blotches and a high, wavy crest; underside in both sexes yellow or orange along the center, fading to pale yellow or white at the edges

Habits Secretive and nocturnal while on land; in water they can often be seen surfacing and displaying to each other during the day

Breeding Fertilization is internal and takes place in the spring; females lay 200–300 single eggs that hatch after 10–20 days

Diet Small invertebrates

Habitat On land they live in damp places, including woods, fields, gardens, and parks; in their aquatic (breeding) phase they use a wide variety of water bodies, including cattle troughs, garden ponds, and the edges of larger lakes

Distribution Central and northern Europe from the British Isles to the Balkans, extending into western Asia north of the Ural Mountains

Status Common

Similar species The palmate newt, *T. helveticus*, is very similar out of the breeding season, and females are almost indistinguishable; several other small newts occur within the same region

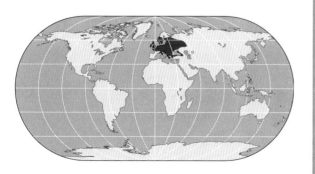

Smooth Newt *Triturus vulgaris*

The smooth newt is the most common newt in much of northern and Central Europe, and is often seen in ditches, village ponds, flooded gravel pits, and garden ponds. Out of the water, however, it is rarely seen unless disturbed while hiding under a log or stone.

SMOOTH NEWTS MAKE their way to breeding ponds in the spring, where they engage in elaborate courtship. Males develop high, wavy-edged crests and brighter colors at this time to attract the females. Once females enter the water, they are pursued by males, who try to position themselves in front of them to block their way. If a female is receptive, the male turns to face her, curls his tail around until it is lying alongside his flank, and vibrates it vigorously. This produces a current of water that carries secretions from his cloaca toward the female and is intended to stimulate her. This stage can last for 30 seconds or more and is sometimes interspersed with other postures and behaviors.

Toward the end of the courtship the male moves backward while still facing the female, and she follows. Then he turns away and walks slowly in front of her, waving his tail. She follows and nuzzles his tail with her snout, which is the cue for him to fold his tail and deposit a spermatophore. In the final act he moves forward while turning sideways again to block her progress. If he has judged correctly, she will now be positioned directly over the spermatophore, which she picks up in her cloaca. The sequence may be repeated several times before the female loses interest and swims away. The male may also need to swim to the surface for air, in which case the sequence ends. Males that can stay submerged for long periods have a better chance of fertilizing females successfully.

Not Just for Decoration

The male's crest may be functional as well as ornamental. In addition to attracting

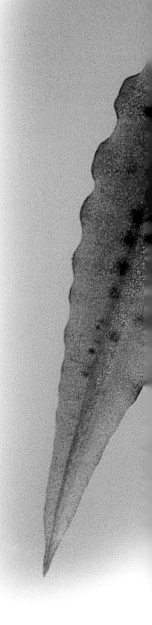

females, it provides a larger surface over which oxygen can be absorbed from the water, thereby increasing the amount of time between each breath. Sometimes a sneaky male, probably one that is smaller and less well endowed than most, waits until the last moment before nipping in and leading the female to his own spermatophore.

Female smooth newts lay 200 to 300 eggs, each individually wrapped in the leaves of water plants and laid at the rate of three to seven a day. The eggs hatch after 10 to 20 days depending on the temperature of the water. After a few days attached to plants, the tiny newt larvae start feeding on microscopic zooplankton. The larvae spend most of their time among the plants and muck at the bottom of the pond, hiding from predators such as dragonfly nymphs, water beetles, fish, and larger newts and newt larvae.

They metamorphose at the end of summer, but some may overwinter, especially if they hatched from eggs that were laid late. Newts that overwinter are larger at metamorphosis and therefore have a better chance of surviving. However, if their ponds dry up, they die. By having an extended season, smooth newts hedge their bets between early metamorphosis and extra growth. Populations that breed in ponds prone to drought tend to produce larvae that develop quickly, but those that breed in more permanent ponds and ditches may have a larger proportion that overwinter.

⊕ Breeding male smooth newts develop brighter colors and a pronounced crest along their back. The females are duller— usually light brown with dark freckles, often with two parallel lines down their back.

Close Relatives

In Britain and much of western Europe the smooth newt's range overlaps with that of the palmate newt, *Triturus helveticus*. However, the palmate newt tends to occur more at higher elevations, probably because upland ponds tend to have softer water, which it prefers. Even so, there are plenty of ponds where both species breed. In other parts of Europe there are a number of very similar species, such as the Italian newt, *T. italicus*, and Bosca's newt, *T. boscai*, which is found in Spain. Another species group within the genus *Triturus* contains several larger, warty species such as the crested newt, *T. cristatus*, and the marbled newt, *T. marmoratus*. The genus as a whole contains 12 species, mostly European, but extending into North Africa and western Asia.

Glossary

Words in SMALL CAPITALS refer to other entries in the glossary.

Acrodont (teeth) teeth attached to the upper edge of the jaw, as opposed to the inside surface (PLEURODONT) or in sockets (THECODONT)

Adaptation a characteristic shape, behavior, or physiological process that equips an organism (or group of related organisms) for its way of life and habitat

Advanced relatively recently evolved (opposite of "primitive")

Albino an animal that has no color pigment in its body and has red eyes

Amniotic egg an egg with a fluid-filled sac within a membrane that encloses the embryo of reptiles, birds, and mammals. Animals that produce amniotic eggs are known as amniotes

Amplexus the position adopted during mating in most frogs and many salamanders, in which the male clasps the female with one or both pairs of limbs. See AXILLARY AMPLEXUS and INGUINAL AMPLEXUS

Annuli the growth rings often visible on the shell of CHELONIANS

Anterior the front part or head and shoulders of an animal

Aposematic coloration bright coloration serving to warn a potential predator that an animal is distasteful or poisonous

Arboreal living in trees or shrubs

Autotomy self-amputation of part of the body. Some lizards practice CAUDAL autotomy: They discard all or part of their tail

Axillary amplexus mating position in frogs in which the male grasps the female behind her front limbs. See INGUINAL AMPLEXUS

Barbel a small, elongated "feeler," or sensory process, on the head, usually of aquatic animals, e.g., some pipid frogs

Binocular vision the ability to focus both eyes on a single subject. The eyes must point forward (not sideways as in most reptiles and amphibians). Binocular vision enables animals, including humans, to judge distances

Bridges the sides of a turtle's shell, attaching to the CARAPACE above and the PLASTRON below

Brille the transparent covering over the eyes of snakes and some lizards, such as geckos

Bromeliad member of a family of plants restricted to the New World. Many live attached to trees, including "urn plants" in which ARBOREAL frogs sometimes breed

Calcareous containing calcium carbonate

Carapace the upper part of the shell of turtles and tortoises, the other parts being the PLASTRON and the BRIDGES. Also used to describe the hard structure covering part of any animal's body

Caudal relating to the tail, as in subcaudal scales beneath a snake's tail and caudal (tail) fin

Chelonian a member of the ORDER Chelonia, containing all reptiles variously known as terrapins, turtles, and tortoises

Chromatophore a specialized cell containing pigment, usually located in the outer layers of the skin

Chromosome a thread-shaped structure consisting largely of genetic material (DNA), found in the nucleus of cells

Cirrus (pl. cirri) a slender, usually flexible appendage on an animal

CITES an international conservation organization: Convention on International Trade in Endangered Species

Class a TAXONOMIC category ranking below PHYLUM, containing a number of ORDERS

Cloaca the common chamber into which the urinary, digestive, and reproductive systems discharge their contents, and which opens to the exterior; from Latin meaning "sewer" or "drain"

Clutch the eggs laid by a female at one time

Continuous breeder an animal that may breed at any time of year

Convergent evolution the effect of unrelated animals looking like each other because they have adapted to similar conditions in similar ways

Coprophagy the practice of eating excrement

Costal relating to the ribs

Costal grooves grooves or folds along the flanks of caecilians and some salamanders that correspond to the position of the ribs

Crocodilian a member of the order Crocodylia, including alligators, caimans, crocodiles, and gharials

Cryptic having the ability to remain hidden, usually by means of camouflage, e.g., cryptic coloration

Cutaneous respiration breathing that takes place across the skin's surface, especially important in amphibians

Cycloid disklike, resembling a circle

Denticle toothlike scale

Dermis layer of skin immediately below the EPIDERMIS

Dewlap flap or fold of skin under an animal's throat. Sometimes used in displays, e.g., in anole lizards

Dimorphism the existence of two distinct forms within a SPECIES, which is then said to be dimorphic. In species in which there are more than two forms, they are polymorphic. See SEXUAL DIMORPHISM

Direct development transition from egg to the adult form in amphibians without passing through a free-living LARVAL stage

Dorsal relating to the back or upper surface of the body or one of its parts

Ectotherm (adj. ectothermic) an animal that relies on external heat sources, such as the sun, to raise its body temperature. Reptiles and amphibians are ectotherms. See ENDOTHERM

Eft juvenile, TERRESTRIAL phase in the life cycle of a newt. The red eft is the terrestrial juvenile form of the eastern newt, *Notophthalmus viridescens*

Egg tooth small toothlike scale that some amphibians and reptiles have on the tip of their snout to assist in breaking through their eggshell

Endemic SPECIES, GENERA, or FAMILIES that are restricted to a particular geographical region

Endotherm (adj. endothermic) an animal that can sustain a high body temperature by means of heat generated within the body by the metabolism. See ECTOTHERM

Epidermis surface layer of the skin of a vertebrate

Epiphyte plant growing on another plant but not a parasite. Includes many orchids and BROMELIADS and some mosses and ferns

Estivation a state of inactivity during prolonged periods of drought or high temperature. During estivation the animal often buries itself in soil or mud. See HIBERNATION

Estuarine living in the lower part of a river (estuary) where fresh water meets and mixes with seawater

Explosive breeder a SPECIES in which the breeding season is very short, resulting in large numbers of animals mating at the same time

External fertilization fusing of eggs and sperm outside the female's body, as in nearly all frogs and toads. See INTERNAL FERTILIZATION

Family TAXONOMIC category ranking below ORDER, containing GENERA that are more closely related to one another than any other grouping of genera

Farming hatching and rearing of young CHELONIANS and CROCODILIANS from a captive-breeding population. See RANCHING

Fauna the animal life of a locality or region

Femoral gland gland situated on an animal's thigh

Femoral pores row of pores along an animal's thighs. Most obvious in many lizards

Fertilization union of an egg and a sperm

Gamete OVUM or sperm

Genus (pl. genera) taxonomic category ranking below FAMILY; a group of SPECIES all more closely related to one another than to any other group of species

Gestation carrying the developing young within the body. Gestation period is the length of time that this occurs

Gill respiratory structure in aquatic animals through which gas exchange takes place

Gill slits slits in which GILLS are situated and present in some amphibians and their LARVAE

Granular (scale) small grainlike scales covering the body, as in some geckos and in the file snakes, *Acrochordus*

Gravid carrying eggs or young

Gular pouch area of expandable skin in the throat region

Hedonic glands glands in a male salamander that stimulate a female when they are rubbed against her body

Heliotherm an animal that basks to regulate body temperature

Hemipenis (pl. hemipenes) one of two grooved copulatory structures present in the males of some reptiles

Herbivore animal that eats plants

Heterogeneous (scales) scales that differ in shape or size. See HOMOGENEOUS (SCALES)

Hibernation a period of inactivity, often spent underground, to avoid extremes of cold. See ESTIVATION

Hinge a means by which the PLASTRON of some CHELONIANS can be pulled up, giving the reptile more protection against a would-be predator

Home range an area in which an animal lives except for MIGRATIONS or rare excursions

Homogeneous (scales) scales that are all the same shape and size. See HETEROGENEOUS (SCALES)

Hyoid "u"-shaped bone at the base of the tongue to which the larynx is attached

Inguinal pertaining to the groin

Inguinal amplexus a mating position in which a male frog or salamander clasps a female around the lower abdomen. See AXILLARY AMPLEXUS

Intergular scute a single plate, or SCUTE, lying between the paired gular scutes on the PLASTRON of side-necked turtles

Internal fertilization fusing of eggs and sperm inside the female's body, as in reptiles and most salamanders. See EXTERNAL FERTILIZATION

Interstitial the thin skin between the scales of reptiles. Sometimes called "interscalar" skin

Introduced species brought from lands where it occurs naturally to lands where it has not previously occurred

IUCN International Union for the Conservation of Nature, responsible for assigning animals and plants to internationally agreed categories of rarity. *See* table below

Jacobson's organ (or vomeronasal organ) one of a pair of grooves extending from the nasal cavity and opening into the mouth cavity in some mammals and reptiles. Molecules collected on the tongue are sampled by this organ, which supplements the sense of smell

Juvenile young animal, not sexually mature

Karst a porous form of limestone

Keeled scales a ridge on the DORSAL scales of some snakes

Keratophagy the practice of eating molted skin

Lamella (pl. lamellae) thin transverse plates across the undersides of the toes of some lizards, especially geckos

Larva (pl. larvae) early stage in the development of an animal (including amphibians) after hatching from the egg

Lateral line organ sense organ embedded in the skin of some aquatic animals, including LARVAL salamanders and some frogs, which responds to waterborne vibrations. Usually arranged in a row along the animal's side

Leucistic an animal that lacks all pigment except that in its eyes. Partially leucistic animals have patches of white over an otherwise normally pigmented skin. See ALBINO

Life cycle complete life history of an organism from one stage to the recurrence of that stage, e.g., egg to egg

Life history history of a single individual organism from the fertilization of the egg until its death

Lifestyle general mode of life of an animal, e.g., NOCTURNAL predator, aquatic HERBIVORE, parasite

Live-bearing giving birth to young that have developed beyond the egg stage. Live-bearers may be VIVIPAROUS or OVOVIVIPAROUS

Lure (noun) part of the body, such as the tail, that is used to entice prey closer

Mental gland gland on the chin of some newts and salamanders that appears to stimulate the female during courtship; one of the HEDONIC GLANDS

Metabolism chemical or energy changes occurring within a living organism that are involved in various life activities

Metamorphosis transformation of an animal from one stage of its life history to another, e.g., from LARVA to adult

Microenvironment local conditions that immediately surround an organism

Migration movement of animals from one place to another, often in large numbers and often for breeding purposes

Mimic an animal that resembles an animal belonging to another SPECIES, usually a distasteful or venomous one, or some inedible object

Milt sperm-containing fluid produced by a male frog during egg laying to fertilize the eggs

Montane pertaining to mountains or SPECIES that live in mountains

Morph form or phase of an animal

Morphological relating to the form and structure of an organism

Nasolabial groove a groove running from the nostril to the upper lip in male plethodontid salamanders

Neonate the newborn young of a live-bearer

Neoteny condition in which a LARVA fails to METAMORPHOSE and retains its larval features as an adult. Species with this condition are said to be neotenic. The axolotl is the best-known example. See PEDOMORPHOSIS

Neotropics the tropical part of the New World, including northern South America, Central America, part of Mexico, and the West Indies

Newt amphibious salamanders of the genera *Triturus, Taricha,* and *Notophthalmus*

Niche the role played by a SPECIES in its particular community. It is determined by its food and temperature preferences; each species' niche within a community is unique

Nocturnal active at night

Nuptial pad an area of dark, rough skin that develops in male amphibians on the hands, arms, or chest of some SPECIES prior to the breeding season. Its purpose is to allow the male to grip the female in AMPLEXUS

Occipital lobe the pyramid-shaped area at the back of the brain that helps an animal interpret vision

Ocular of the eye

Olfactory relating to the sense of smell

Omnivore an animal that eats both animal and plant material

Order taxonomic category ranking below CLASS and above FAMILY

Osteoderm small bone in the skin of some reptiles; lies under the scales

Ovary female gonad or reproductive organ that produces the OVUM

Overwinter survive the winter

Oviduct the duct in females that carries the OVUM from the ovary to the CLOACA

Oviparous reproducing by eggs that hatch outside the female's body

IUCN CATEGORIES

EX **Extinct**, when there is no reasonable doubt that the last individual of the species has died

EW **Extinct in the Wild**, when a species is known only to survive in captivity or as a naturalized population well outside the past range.

CR **Critically Endangered**, when a species is facing an extremely high risk of extinction in the wild in the immediate future.

EN **Endangered**, when a species is facing a very high risk of extinction in the wild in the near future.

VU **Vulnerable**, when a species is facing a high risk of extinction in the wild in the medium-term future.

LR **Lower Risk**, when a species has been evaluated and does not satisfy the criteria for CR, EN, or VU.

DD **Data Deficient**, when there is not enough information about a species to assess the risk of extinction.

NE **Not Evaluated**, species that have not been assessed by the IUCN criteria.

Ovoviviparous reproducing by eggs that the female retains within her body until they hatch; the developing eggs contain a yolk sac but receive no nourishment from the mother through a placenta or similar structure

Ovum (pl. ova) female germ cell or GAMETE; an egg cell or egg

Papilla (pl. papillae) aised projection(s) of soft tissue often seen on the head and neck of aquatic CHELONIANS

Parietal eye a VESTIGIAL eye situated in the top of the head of tuataras and some lizards, sometimes known as the "third eye"

Parietals pairs of bones forming the rear of the roof of the brain case

Parotid glands pair of large glands on the shoulder, neck, or behind the eye in some salamanders and toads

Parthenogenesis a form of asexual reproduction in which the OVUM develops without being fertilized. Such SPECIES are said to be parthenogenetic

Parturition the process of giving birth to live young

Pectoral girdle the skeleton supporting the forelimbs of a land vertebrate

Pedogenesis form of reproduction by an animal still showing LARVAL characteristics

Pedomorphosis the retention of immature or LARVAL characteristics, such as GILLS, by animals that are sexually mature. See NEOTENY

Permeable property of a substance, such as skin, allowing another substance, such as water, to pass through it

Pheromone a substance released by an organism to induce a response in another individual of the same SPECIES, such as sexual attraction

Phylum taxonomic category ranking above CLASS and below kingdom

Pigment a substance that gives color to part or all of an organism's body

Plastron the ventral portion, or underside, of the shell of a turtle

Pleurodont teeth teeth that are attached to the inside surface of the jaw, as opposed to the upper edge (ACRODONT) or in sockets (THECODONT)

Pond-type larva salamander LARVA with high fins and a deep body, adapted to living in still water. See STREAM-TYPE LARVA

Preanal pores chemical- or pheromone-secreting pores in front of the CLOACA, usually in lizards

Prehensile adapted for grasping or clasping, especially by wrapping around, such as the tail of chameleons

Preocular relating to the front of the eye

Ranching artificial incubation of eggs collected from the wild followed by captive-rearing of the young. A method used with both CHELONIANS and CROCODILIANS to increase population numbers, carried out in an environment free from predators

Rectilinear locomotion a form of movement used by heavy-bodied snakes in which the body progresses in a straight line

Riffle agitated water flowing over rocks or gravel in shallow streams or rivers

Rostral processes extensions to the snout, including horns and other ornamentation

Salt glands glands located in the vicinity of the eye that allow marine turtles and some CROCODILIANS to excrete excessive salt from their bodies, helping prevent them from becoming dehydrated in the marine environment

Satellite male a male frog that does not call but sits near a calling male and intercepts females attracted to the calling male

Savanna open grasslands with scattered trees and bushes, usually in warm areas

Scute enlarged scale on a reptile, including the colorful scales that cover the shell of turtles; divided into different groups, such as the vertebral scutes that run above the VERTEBRAL COLUMN

Sexual dimorphism the existence of marked morphological differences between males and females

Species taxonomic category ranking below GENUS; a group of organisms with common attributes capable of interbreeding and producing healthy fertile offspring

Spermatheca a pouch or sac in the female reproductive tract in which sperm are stored

Spermatophore a structure containing sperm that is passed from the male to the female in some animals, such as in many salamanders

Stream-type larva streamlined LARVA with low fins and elongated body, adapted for living in flowing water. See POND-TYPE LARVA

Subcaudal beneath the tail, as in "subcaudal" scales. See CAUDAL

Subocular usually refers to scales below the eye. See PREOCULAR

Subspecies a locally distinct group of animals that differ slightly from the normal appearance of the SPECIES; often called a race

Substrate the solid material on which an organism lives, e.g., sand, mud, etc.

Suture the zigzag patterning formed beneath the SCUTES where the bones of a CHELONIAN's shell fuse together

Tadpole LARVAL stage of a frog or toad

Talus slopes slopes covered with loose rocks and slabs. Also known as scree

Taxonomy the science of classification: the arrangement of animals and plants into groups based on their natural relationships

Temporal relating to the area between the eye and ear

Terrestrial living on land

Territorial defending an area so as to exclude other members of the same SPECIES

Territory an area that one or more animals defends against other members of the same SPECIES

Thecodont teeth growing in sockets. See ACRODONT

Thermoregulate to expose to or move away from a heat source in order to maintain desired body temperature

Thermoregulation control of body temperature by behavioral or physiological means, so that it maintains a constant or near-constant value

Thyroid gland a gland lying in the neck that produces the hormone THYROXINE

Thyroxine a hormone containing iodine that is involved in a variety of physiological processes, including METAMORPHOSIS in amphibians

Toad any stout-bodied, warty-skinned frog, especially one living away from water. The term has no TAXONOMIC basis, although members of the FAMILY Bufonidae are often called toads

Tongue-flicking constant use of the tongue by snakes and some lizards when exploring their surroundings. Used in conjunction with JACOBSON'S ORGAN

Tubercle a small, knoblike projection

Turtle any shelled reptile, including tortoises and terrapins

Tympanum (pl. tympana) eardrum

Unisexual species a SPECIES consisting only of females, in which reproduction is by PARTHENOGENESIS

Unken reflex a defensive posture shown by some amphibians when attacked, in which the body is arched inward with the head and tail lifted upward. Its purpose is to display a brightly colored underside

Uterine milk a uterine secretion that provides developing embryos with nourishment

Vent the CLOACAL opening of the body. Measurements of reptiles and amphibians are often given as "snout-vent" lengths or simply "s-v" lengths

Ventral describing the lower surface of the body or one of its parts

Vertebral column the spinal skeleton, or backbone, consisting of a series of vertebrae extending from the skull to the tip of the tail

Vertebrate a member of the subphylum Vertebrata, comprising all animals with a VERTEBRAL COLUMN, including fish, amphibians, reptiles, birds, and mammals

Vestigial smaller and of more simple structure than in an evolutionary ancestor. In reptiles and amphibians often used to describe limbs that have become reduced in size through the evolutionary process

Viviparous giving birth to living young that develop within and are nourished by the mother. Often used incorrectly, however, to describe any live-bearing species. See also OVOVIVIPAROUS

Volar pores pores on the underside of the feet

Webbing folds of skin present between the toes of both CROCODILIANS and aquatic CHELONIANS

Xeric adapted to life in an extremely dry habitat

Yolk sac a large sac containing stored nutrients, present in the embryos of fish, amphibians, reptiles, and birds

Further Reading

General

Includes regional guides that contain useful general information. Note that many of these titles are mostly about reptiles, frogs, and toads, but some include a small number of salamanders or caecilians.

Arnold, E. N., *A Field Guide to the Reptiles and Amphibians of Britain and Europe*, Harper Collins, London, 2002

Behler, J. L., and King, F. W., *The Audubon Society Field Guide to North American Reptiles and Amphibians*, Alfred A. Knopf, New York, 1979

Cei, J. M., *Amphibians of Argentina*, Monitore Zoologica Italiano (Italian Journal of Zoology), Monografia number 2, Florence, 1980

Channing, A., *Amphibians of Central and Southern Africa*, Comstock Publishing Associates, Ithaca and London, 2001

Cogger, H. G., *Reptiles and Amphibians of Australia*, 6th edn., Reed New Holland, Sydney, 2000

Duellman, W. E., and Trueb, L., *Biology of Amphibians*, Johns Hopkins University Press, Baltimore, MA, 1994

Glaw, F., and Vences, M., *A Field Guide to the Reptiles and Amphibians of Madagascar*, 2nd edn., published by the authors, Bonn, 1994

Grismer, L. L., *Amphibians and Reptiles of Baja California*, University of California Press, Berkeley, CA, 2002

Halliday, T., and Adler, C. (eds.), *The New Encyclopedia of Reptiles and Amphibians*, Firefly Books, New York and Toronto/Oxford University Press, Oxford, 2002

McCranie, J. R., and Wilson, L. D., *The Amphibians of Honduras*, Society for the Study of Amphibians and Reptiles, Ithaca, NY, 2002

Murphy, J. B., Adler, K., and Collins, J. T. (eds.), *Captive Management and Conservation of Reptiles and Amphibians*, Society for the Study of Amphibians and Reptiles, Ithaca, New York, 1994

Savage, J. M., *Amphibians and Reptiles of Costa Rica*, University of Chicago Press, Chicago, 2002

Schleich, H. H., Kästle, W., and Kabisch, K., *Amphibians and Reptiles of North Africa*, Koeltz Scientific Books, Koenigstien, 1996

Stebbins, R. C., and Cohen, N. W., *A Natural History of Amphibians*, Princeton University Press, Princeton, NJ, 1995

Zug, G. R., Vitt, L. J., and Caldwell, J. P., *Herpetology: An Introductory Biology of Reptiles and Amphibians*, 2nd edn., Academic Press, San Diego, 2001

Specific to this volume

Bishop, S. C., *Handbook of Salamanders*, Cornell University Press, Ithaca, NY, 1994

Griffiths, R. A., *Newts and Salamanders of Europe*, T. and A. D. Poyser Ltd, London, 1996

Nickerson, M. A., and Mays, C. E., *The Hellbenders*, Milwaukee Public Museum, Milwaukee, WI, 1972

Petranka, J. W., *Salamanders of the United States and Canada*, Smithsonian Institute Press, Washington DC and London, 1998

Useful Websites

General

Frost, Darrel R. 2004. Amphibian Species of the World: an Online Reference. Version 3.0 (22 August, 2004). Electronic Database accessible at: **http://research.amnh.org/herpetology/amphibia/index.php** American Museum of Natural History, New York, USA

Myers, P. 2001. "Vertebrata" (Online), Animal Diversity. Accessible at: **http://animaldiversity.ummz.umich.edu/site/accounts/information/ Amphibia.html**

http://elib.cs.berkeley.edu/aw/index.html
AmphibiaWeb, a site inspired by global amphibian declines, is an online system that allows free access to information on amphibian biology and conservation. Lists all known species of amphibians and gives species accounts, photographs, and distribution maps to some. New material is added constantly

http://www.globalamphibians.org/index.html
The Global Amphibian Assessment (GAA) is the first-ever comprehensive assessment of the conservation status of the world's 5,743 known species of frogs, toads, salamanders, and caecilians. This website presents results of the assessments, including IUCN Red List threat category, range map, ecology information, and other data for every amphibian species

http://www.herplit.com/
A listing of herpetological literature, including older material

http://www.kingsnake.com
Many pages about reptiles and amphibians, especially their care in captivity, and links to other organizations

http://www.livingunderworld.org/caudata/
A growing database of information about amphibians

http://www.mabnetamericas.org/species/amphibia.html
A straightforward checklist of all families, genera, and species of amphibians

http://www.open.ac.uk/daptf/index.htm
The website of the Declining Amphibian Populations Task Force gives information about endangered species of amphibians across the world

http://research.amnh.org/herpetology/amphibia/index.html
"Amphibian Species of the World." A catalogue of all amphibian species with synonyms and additional information, accessed with a good search engine

http://www.redlist.org
IUCN Red List gives details of all threatened animals, including reptiles and amphibians

http://www.si.edu/resource/faq/nmnh/zoology.htm#vz
General information about reptiles and amphibians and links to many educational sites

http://tolweb.org/tree?group=Living_Amphibians&contgroup=Terrestrial_Vertebrates
A collaborative Internet project produced by biologists from around the world, containing information about the diversity of organisms on earth, their history, and characteristics. All vertebrates are covered. The link given takes you straight to amphibians

Specific to this volume

http://www.caecilian.org/
A good source of information about caecilians

http://www.caudata.org/
An extensive website with information about caudates (newts and salamanders) throughout the world

http://www.caudata.org/cc/
A section of the above website dealing with newts and salamanders in captivity

http://hellbenders.sanwalddesigns.com/index.shtml
The hellbender home page, dedicated to the conservation of North American giant salamanders

Set Index

A **bold** number shows the volume and is followed by the relevant page numbers (e.g., **21**: 52, 74).

Common names in **bold** (e.g., **adder**) mean that the animal has an illustrated main entry in the set. Underlined page numbers (e.g., **29**: 78–79) refer to the main entry for that animal.

Italic page numbers (e.g., **22**: *103*) point to illustrations of animals in parts of the set other than the main entry.

Page numbers in parentheses—e.g., **21**: (24)—locate information in At-a-Glance boxes.

Animals that have main entries in the set are indexed under their common names, alternative common names, and scientific names.

121

Picture Credits

Abbreviations

A Ardea, London; BCL Bruce Coleman Limited; CM Chris Mattison; FLPA Frank Lane Picture Agency; NHPA Natural History Photographic Agency; NPL Naturepl.com; PW Premaphotos Wildlife; P.com/OSF Photolibrary.com/Oxford Scientific Films; SPL Science Photo Library

t = top; **b** = bottom; **c** = center; **l** = left; **r** = right

Jacket: tl Geoff Trinder/A; **tr** Martin Harvey/NHPA; **bl** John Cancalosi/A; **br** Marty Cordano/P.com/OSF

8–9 Zig Leszczynski/P.com/OSF; **13** John Cancalosi, Okapia/P.com/OSF; **14–15** Michael Fogden/P.com/OSF; **16** Agence France Presse; **17** Daniel Heuclin/NHPA; **18**, **18–19**, **20–21** CM; **22** Daniel Heuclin/NHPA; **23** E.& D. Hosking/FLPA; **24–25** CM; **27** Jose Ruiz/NPL; **28–29** T. Kitchin & V. Hurst/NHPA; **29** Fabio Liverani/NPL; **31** Daniel Heuclin/NHPA; **32–33** Pat Morris/A; **34–35** David M. Dennis/P.com/OSF; **36–37** Nigel Marven/NPL; **39** Professor Jack Dermid/P.com/OSF; **40–41** Gary Braasch/Corbis; **42–43** Karl Switak/NHPA; **44–45** Minden Pictures/FLPA; **47** Professor Jack Dermid/P.com/OSF; **49t**, **49b** Daniel Heuclin/NHPA; **51** David M. Dennis/P.com/OSF; **53** Ron Austing/FLPA; **55** Professor Jack Dermid/P.com/OSF; **57t** S. & D. & K. Maslowski/FLPA; **57b** Jim Zipp/A; **59** Zig Leszczynski, AA/P.com/OSF; **60–61** CM; **62–63** Stephen Dalton/NHPA; **65** CM; **66–67** Marty Cordano/P.com/OSF; **67** Raymond Gehman/Corbis; **68–69** Michael Fogden/P.com/OSF; **69** David M. Dennis/P.com/OSF; **70** Zig Leszczynski/P.com/OSF; **71** Minden Pictures/FLPA; **72–73** David M. Dennis/P.com/OSF; **75** Zig Leszczynski/P.com/OSF; **76–77** Michael Fogden/P.com/OSF; **77** Phil Savoie/NPL; **78–79** Raymond Mendez/P.com/OSF; **79** Zig Liszczynski/P.com/OSF; **80–81** CM; **83** Nature's Images Inc. **85** CM; **86–87** Zig Leszczynski/P.com/OSF; **88–89** Fabio Liverani/NPL; **90** David Welling/NPL; **91** CM; **93** Jose B.Ruis/NPL; **95** CM; **97** Daniel Heuclin/NHPA; **99** Professor Jack Dermid/P.com/OSF; **101** CM; **103** Martin Gabriel/NPL; **104**, **105** CM; **106** Daniel Heuclin/NHPA; **109** Dave Sarver, AA/P.com/OSF; **111** CM